Reach Your

SCORPIO

Teresa Moorey

Dedication

To my friends Jane and Annie, Scorpios of intensity and compassion

Orders: please contact Bookpoint Ltd, 39 Milton Park, Abingdon, Oxon OX14 4TD. Telephone: (44) 01235 400414, Fax: (44) 01235 400454. Lines are open from 9.00–6.00, Monday to Saturday, with a 24 hour message answering service. Email address: orders@bookpoint.co.uk

British Library Cataloguing in Publication Data
A catalogue record for this title is available from The British Library

ISBN 0 340 69716 4

First published 1998
Impression number 11   10   9   8   7   6   5   4   3   2
Year   2004   2003   2002   2001   2000   1999   1998

Copyright © 1998 Teresa Moorey

All rights reserved. No part of this publication may be reproduced or transmitted in any form or by any means, electronic or mechanical, including photocopy, recording, or any information storage and retrieval system, without permission in writing from the publisher or under licence from the Copyright Licensing Agency Limited. Further details of such licences (for reprographic reproduction) may be obtained from the Copyright Licensing Agency Limited, of 90 Tottenham Court Road, London W1P 9HE.

Typeset by Transet Limited, Coventry, England.
Printed in Great Britain for Hodder & Stoughton Educational, a division of Hodder Headline plc, 338 Euston Road, London NW1 3BH by Cox and Wyman, Reading, Berks.

Contents

INTRODUCTION		1
PARANOID, OBSCURE OR POWERFUL – WHAT SORT OF SCORPIO ARE YOU?		12
Chapter 1	THE ESSENTIAL SCORPIO	17
	The power and the passion	17
	Scorpio body language	18
	Myths of the Scorpion	18
	Element, Quality and Ruling Planet	20
	Magicians and sex maniacs	23
	Old laser-eyes	25
	The worm in the apple	26
	Nothing in moderation	27
	The frog and the scorpion	28
Chapter 2	RELATIONSHIPS	30
	Scorpio sexuality	31
	The wishes of Savitri	33
	Scorpio woman in love	35
	Scorpio man in love	37
	Gay Scorpio	38
	Scorpio love traps	39
	Scorpio and marriage	41
	When love walks out – how Scorpio copes	42
Chapter 3	ALL IN THE FAMILY	45
	Scorpio mother	45
	Scorpio father	47
	The Scorpio child	48

♏ SCORPIO ♏

	Scorpio as sibling	52
	Scorpio in the home	52
Chapter 4	FRIENDSHIPS AND THE SINGLE LIFE	55
	Scorpio as a friend	55
	Scorpio and the single life	57
Chapter 5	CAREER	60
	Traditional Scorpio careers	61
	What to look for in your work	61
	The Sphynx	62
	The Black Widow	63
	The Scorpio boss	64
	The Scorpio employee	65
	When unemployment strikes	66
	Self-employment and other matters	67
Chapter 6	HEALTHY, WEALTHY – AND WISE?	69
	Health	69
	Money	71
	Wisdom	72
Chapter 7	STYLE AND LEISURE	74
	Your leisure	74
	Your style	76
Appendix 1	SCORPIO COMBINED WITH MOON SIGN	79
Appendix 2	ZODIACAL COMPATIBILITY	88
	SCORPIO COMPATIBILITIES	89
Appendix 3	TRADITIONAL ASSOCIATIONS AND TOTEM	102
FURTHER READING AND RESOURCES		106

Introduction

A PERSPECTIVE OF ASTROLOGY

Interest in the mystery and significance of the heavens is perhaps as old as humanity. If we can cast our imaginations back, to a time when there were no street lamps, televisions or even books, if we can picture how it must have been to have nothing to do through the deep nights of winter other than to sit and weave stories by the fire at the cave mouth, then we can come close to sensing how important the great dome of stars must have seemed in ancient times.

We are prone to believe that we are wiser today, having progressed beyond old superstitions. We know that all stars are like our Sun – giant nuclear reactors. We know that the planets are lumps of rock reflecting sunlight, they are not gods or demons. But how wise are we in truth? Our growing accumulation of facts brings us no closer to discovering the real meaning behind life. It may well be that our cave-dwelling ancestors knew better than us the meaning of holism. The study of astrology may be part of a journey towards a more holistic perception, taking us, as it does, through the fertile, and often uncharted realms of our own personality.

Until the seventeenth century astrology (which searches for the meaning of heavenly patterns) and astronomy (which seeks to clarify facts about the skies) were one, and it was the search for meanings, not facts that inspired the earliest investigations. Lunar phases have been found carved on bone and stone figures from as early as 15,000BCE (Before Common Era). Astrology then evolved through the civilisations of Mesopotamia and Greece among others.

♏ SCORPIO ♏

Through the 'dark ages' much astrological lore was preserved in Islamic countries, but in the fifteenth century astrology grew in popularity in the West. Queen Elizabeth I had her own personal astrologer, John Dee, and such fathers of modern astronomy as Kepler and Galileo served as court astrologers in Europe.

Astrology was taught at the University of Salamanca until 1776. What is rarely appreciated is that some of our greatest scientists, notably Newton and even Einstein, were led to their discoveries by intuition. Newton was a true mystic, and it was the search for meaning – the same motivation that inspired the Palaeolithic observer – that gave rise to some of our most brilliant advances. Indeed Newton is widely believed to have been an astrologer. The astronomer Halley, who discovered the famous comet, is reported to have criticised Newton for this, whereupon Sir Isaac replied 'I have studied it Sir, you have not!'

During the twentieth century astrology enjoyed a revival, and in 1948 The Faculty of Astrological Studies was founded, offering tuition of high quality and an examination system. The great psychologist Carl Jung was a supporter of astrology, and his work has expanded ideas about the mythic connections of the birth chart. Astrology is still eyed askance by many people, and there is no doubt that there is little purely scientific corroboration for astrology – the exception to this is the exhaustive statistical work undertaken by the Gauquelins. Michel Gauquelin was a French statistician whose research shows undeniable connection between professional prominence and the position of planets at birth. Now that the concept of a mechanical universe is being superseded, there is a greater chance that astrology and astronomy will reunite.

Anyone who consults a good astrologer comes away deeply impressed by the insight of the birth chart. Often it is possible to see very deeply into the personality and to be able to throw light on current dilemmas. It is noteworthy that even the most sceptical of people tend to know their Sun sign and the characteristics associated with it.

■ WHAT IS A BIRTH CHART?

Your birth chart is a map of the heavens drawn up for the time, date and place of your birth. An astrologer will prefer you to be as accurate as you can about the time of day, for that affects the sign rising on the eastern horizon. This 'rising sign' is very important to your personality. However, if you do not know your birth time a chart can still be compiled for you. There will be some details missing, but useful interpretations may still be made. It is far better for the astrologer to know that your birth time is in question than to operate from a position of false certainty. The birth chart for Dylan Thomas (page 4) is a simplified chart. Additional factors would be entered on the chart and considered by an astrologer, such as angles (aspects) between the planets, and the houses.

The birth chart shows each of the planets and the Moon in the astrological signs, and can be thought of as an 'energy map' of the different forces operating within the psyche. Thus the Sun sign (often called 'birth sign' or 'star sign') refers only to the position of the Sun. If the planets are in very different signs from the Sun sign, the interpretation will be greatly modified. Thus, if a person has Sun in Leo yet is somewhat introverted or quiet, this may be because the Moon was in reserved Capricorn when that person was born. Nonetheless, the Sun represents the light of consciousness, the integrating force, and most people recognise that they are typical of their Sun sign, although in some people it will be more noticeable than in others. The planets Mercury and Venus are very close to the Sun and often occupy the same sign, so intensifying the Sun-sign influence.

♏ SCORPIO ♏

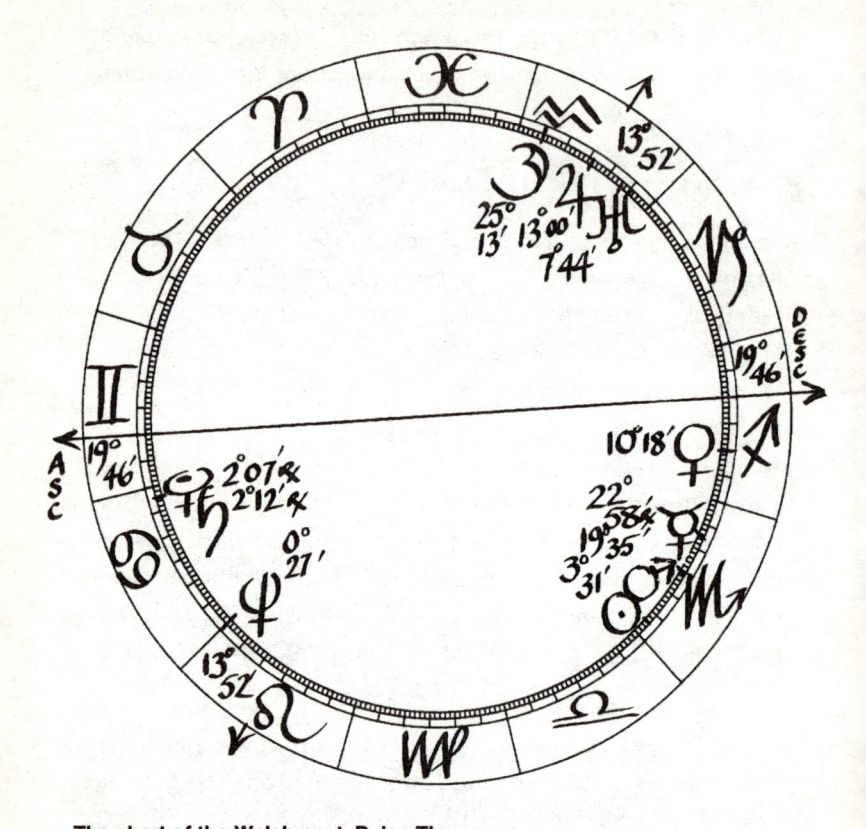

The chart of the Welsh poet, Dylan Thomas
Thomas has Sun ☉, Mars ♂ and Mercury ☿ in Scorpio, showing the depth and passion he bought to his creativity.

This book is written about your Sun sign, because the Sun sign serves as an accessible starting point for those wishing to learn about themselves through astrology. However, do not let your interest stop there. If you find anything helpful in comments and advice stemming from Sun sign alone, you will find your true birth chart even more revealing. The address of the Faculty of Astrological

♏ Introduction ♏

The **planets** are life principles, energy centres. To enable you to understand the birth chart, here are their glyphs:

Sun	☉	Jupiter	♃
Moon	☽	Saturn	♄
Mercury	☿	Uranus	♅
Venus	♀	Neptune	♆
Mars	♂	Pluto	♀ (♇)

Rising Sign or **Ascendant** (**ASC**) is the way we have of meeting the world, our outward persona. **Midheaven** (**MC**) refers to our image, aspirations, how we like to be seen.

The **signs** are modes of expression, ways of being. Here are their glyphs:

Aries	♈	Libra	♎
Taurus	♉	Scorpio	♏
Gemini	♊	Sagittarius	♐
Cancer	♋	Capricorn	♑
Leo	♌	Aquarius	♒
Virgo	♍	Pisces	♓

Using knowledge of the glyphs you can see that the Sun is in Scorpio in our example birth chart (page 4).

Studies appears in 'Further Reading and Resources' at the back of this book, and it is a good idea to approach them for a list of trained astrologers who can help you. Moon *phase* at birth (as distinct from Moon sign) is also very important. *The Moon and You for Beginners* (see 'Further Reading') explains this fascinating area clearly, and provides a simple chart for you to look up your Moon phase, and learn what this means for your personality.

♏ SCORPIO ♏

■ HOW DOES ASTROLOGY WORK?

We cannot explain astrology by the usual methods of cause and effect. In fact, there are many things we cannot explain. No one can define exactly what life is. We do not know exactly what electricity is, but we know how to use it. Few of us have any idea how a television set works, but we know how to turn it on. Although we are not able to explain astrology we are still able to use it, as any capable astrologer will demonstrate.

Jung discovered something called 'synchronicity'. This he defined as 'an acausal connecting principle'. Simply, this means that some events have a meaningful connection *other than cause and effect*. The planets do not cause us to do things, but their movements are synchronistic with our lives. The old dictum 'as above, so below' applies here. It is a mystery. We can't explain it, but that doesn't mean we should refuse to believe in it. A little boy on a visit to the circus saw an elephant for the first time and said 'There's no such thing'. We may laugh at the little boy, but how many of us respond to things we do not understand in this way?

The planetary positions in your birth chart are synchronistic with the time of your birth, when you took on separate existence, and they are synchronistic with your individuality in this life. They have much to say about you.

■ MYTH AND PSYCHOLOGY

The planets are named after the old gods and goddesses of Rome, which in turn link in with Greek and other pantheons. The planets represent 'life principles' – forces that drive the personality, and as such they can be termed 'archetypal'. This means that they are basic ideas, universal within human society and are also relevant in terms of the forces that, in some inexplicable way, inhabit the corners of the universe and inform the Earth and all human

Introduction

institutions. Thus the assertive energy that is represented by Mars means energetic action of all sorts – explosions and fires, wars, fierce debates and personal anger. Put briefly, here are the meanings of the planets:

- Mercury – intellect and communication
- Venus – love, unifying, relating
- Mars – assertion, energy, fighting spirit
- Jupiter – expansion, confidence, optimism
- Saturn – limitation, discipline
- Uranus – rebellion, independence
- Neptune – power to seek the ideal, sense the unseen
- Pluto – power to transform and evolve

These principles are modified according to the astrological sign they inhabit; thus Venus in Pisces may be gently loving, dreamy and self-sacrificing, while Venus in Aries will be demanding and adventurous in relationships. Thus the planets in signs form a complex psychological framework – and that is only part of the story of chart interpretation!

In the old mythologies these 'energies' or 'archetypes' or 'gods' were involved in classical dramas. An example is the story of Saturn and Uranus. Uranus is the rejecting father of Saturn, who later castrates and murders his father – thus innovative people reject reactionaries, who then murder them, so the revolutionary part of the personality is continually 'killed off' by the restrictive part. The exact positions and angles between the planets will indicate how this and other myths may come to life. In addition, the mere placement of planets by sign – and, of course, especially the Sun sign, call forth various myths as illustrations. The ancient myths are good yarns, but they are also inspired and vivid dramatisations of what may be going on repeatedly within your personality and that of your nearest and dearest. Myths are used by many modern psychologists and therapists in a tradition that has grown since Jung. We shall be using mythic themes to illustrate internal dynamics in this book.

♏ SCORPIO ♏

■ THE SIGNS OF THE ZODIAC

There are twelve signs, and each of these belongs to an Element – Earth, Fire, Air or Water, and a Quality – Cardinal, Fixed or Mutable. The Cardinal signs are more geared to action, the Fixed tend to remain stable and rooted, whereas the Mutable signs are adaptable, changeable.

SIGN	QUALITY	ELEMENT
Aries	Cardinal	Fire
Taurus	Fixed	Earth
Gemini	Mutable	Air
Cancer	Cardinal	Water
Leo	Fixed	Fire
Virgo	Mutable	Earth
Libra	Cardinal	Air
Scorpio	Fixed	Water
Sagittarius	Mutable	Fire
Capricorn	Cardinal	Earth
Aquarius	Fixed	Air
Pisces	Mutable	Water

Jung defined four functions of consciousness – four different ways of perceiving the world – 'thinking', 'feeling', 'sensation' and 'intuition'. Thinking is the logical, evaluative approach that works in terms of the mind. Feeling is also evaluative, but this time in relation to culture and family needs. This is not the same as emotion, although 'feeling' people often process emotions more smoothly than other types. Jung saw 'feeling' as rational, too. 'Sensation' refers to the 'here and now', the five physical senses, while 'intuition' relates to the possible, to visions and hunches. Jung taught that we tend to have one function uppermost in conscious-

Introduction

ness, another one or maybe two secondary and another repressed or 'inferior', although we all possess each of these functions to some degree.

Jungian ideas are being refined and expanded, and they are incorporated into modern methods of personality testing, as in the Myers-Briggs test. If a prospective employer has recently given you such a test, it was to establish your talents and potential for the job. However, the basic four-fold division is still extremely useful, and I find it is often of great help in assisting clients to understand themselves, and their partners, in greater depth – for we are all apt to assume that everyone processes information and applies it in the same way as we do. But they don't! It is worthy of mention that the important categories of 'introverted' and 'extraverted' were also identified by Jung. In astrology, Fire and Air signs seem to be extraverted, generally speaking, and Earth and Water introverted – and this has been borne out by the statistical research of the astrologer, Jeff Mayo. However, this doesn't mean that all feeling and sensation people are introverted and all intuitives and thinkers extraverted – this is definitely not the case, and calls for more detailed examination of the chart (e.g. lots of Fire and Water may mean an extravert feeling type).

Very broadly speaking we may link the Fire signs to intuition, Water to feeling, Earth to sensation and Air to thinking. Often thinking and feeling are drawn together and sensation and intuition are attracted, because they are opposites. This probably happens because we all seek to become more whole, but the process can be painful. The notion of the four functions, when understood, does help to throw light on some of the stumbling blocks we often encounter in relationships. However, some people just do not seem to fit. Also Fire doesn't always correspond to intuition, Water to feeling, etc. – it seems this is usually the case, but not all astrologers agree. Some link Fire with feeling, Water with intuition, and most agree that other chart factors are also important. As with all theories, this can be used to help, expand and clarify, not as a rigid system to impose definitions. We shall be learning more about these matters in relation to the Sun sign in the following pages.

■ THE PRECESSION OF THE EQUINOXES

One criticism often levelled at astrology is that 'the stars have moved' and so the old signs are invalid. There is some truth in this, and it is due to a phenomenon called 'The Precession of the Equinoxes'. The beginning of the sign Aries occurs when the Sun is overhead at the equator, moving northwards. This is called the Spring Equinox, for now day and night are equal all over the globe, and the first point of Aries is called the 'equinoctial point'. Because the Earth not only turns on its axis but 'rocks' on it (imagine a giant knitting needle driven through the poles – the Earth spins on this, but the head of the needle also slowly describes a circle in space) the equinoctial point has moved against the background of stars. Thus, when the Sun is overhead at the equator, entering Aries, it is no longer at the start of the constellation of Aries, where it occurred when the signs were named, but is now in the constellation of Pisces. The equinoctial point is moving backwards into Aquarius, hence the idea of the dawning 'Aquarian age'.

So where does that leave astrology? Exactly in the same place, in actuality. For it all depends on how you think the constellations came to be named in the first place. Did our ancestors simply look up and see the shape of a Ram in the sky? Or did they – being much more intuitive and in tune with their surroundings than we are – feel sharply aware of the quality, the energies around at a certain time of the year, and *then* look skyward, translating what they sensed into a suitable starry symbol? This seems much more likely – and you have only to look at the star groups to see that it takes a fair

♏ Introduction ♏

bit of imagination to equate most of them with the figures they represent! The Precession of the Equinoxes does not affect astrological interpretation, for it is based upon observation and intuition, rather than 'animals in the sky'.

USING THIS BOOK

Reach Your Potential – Scorpio explores your Sun sign and what this means in terms of your personality; the emphasis is on self-exploration. All the way through, hints are given to help you to begin to understand yourself better, ask questions about yourself and use what you have to maximum effect. This book will show you how to use positive Scorpion traits to your best advantage, and how to neutralise negative Scorpion traits. Don't forget that by reading it you are consenting, however obliquely, to the notion that you are connected in strange and mysterious ways to the web of the cosmos. What happens within you is part of a meaningful pattern that you can explore and become conscious of, thereby acquiring greater influence on the course of your life. Let this encourage you to ask further questions.

Some famous Scorpios

George Eliot, Prince Charles, Marie Antoinette, Richard Burton, Madame Curie, Charles de Gaulle, Marie Dressler, Indira Gandhi, Billy Graham, Hetty Greene, Grace Kelly, Katharine Hepburn, Robert Kennedy, Vivien Leigh, Martin Luther, Margaret Mead, Marianne Moore, Pablo Picasso, Theodore Roosevelt, Fenella Fielding, Nigel Dempster, Dylan Thomas, Auguste Rodin, Mata Hari, Robert Oppenheimer.

Scorpios in public life bring an intensity of commitment to all they undertake, and may be reformers or innovators who strike at the root of matters, or memorable and dramatic personalities.

♏ SCORPIO ♏

Paranoid, obscure or powerful – what sort of Scorpio are you?

Here is a quiz to give an idea of how you are operating at the moment. Its tone is light-hearted, but the intent is serious and you may find out something interesting about yourself. Don't think too hard about the answers, just pick the one that appeals to you most.

1. **At a party someone you know only slightly is obviously aware that you have a guilty secret. How do you react?**

    a) ❏ You make sure that you stay sober for the rest of the evening, plying everyone with probing questions as they get the worse for drink, until you are armed with lots of information so you can get back at the guilty party.

    b) ❏ You know where that information came from. You make up your mind to keep more to yourself in future.

    c) ❏ So what if they know that? You can tell just by looking around who's got a hidden agenda – and who fancies you rotten. Things should be interesting later . . .

2. **Which saying most strikes a chord?**

    a) ❏ 'Better to reign in hell than serve in heaven.'

    b) ❏ 'Walk softly and carry a big stick.'

    c) ❏ 'Where there's fear there's power.'

3. **Something in the manner of your lover isn't quite 'right' and you wonder if his or her feelings have changed or if there is someone else. What do you do?**

    a) ❏ Now begins the dirty trek through pockets, briefcase, diary. Finding nothing, you set traps.

Introduction

b) ☐ You go silent and withdrawn – no sex, no nothing. You'll show him or her.

c) ☐ You aren't quite sure what the matter is but you can cope with anything if you know what it is. You plan a quiet time to confront the matter.

4. **You were about to put in a report to your boss about some innovations when you find a colleague has got there first.**

    a) ☐ You make it your business to find out everything about this person. You'll get even somehow.

    b) ☐ You resolve to lock your desk even when you go to coffee (as well as at lunch and night-time). If you get promotion your colleague may as well pack his or her bags.

    c) ☐ How did this happen? Was it coincidence/telepathy? You suggest you have a drink together to find out.

5. **You pass a beggar, hunched on a tattered blanket at the street corner, arm over a bag of bones that looks like a dog. What do you do?**

    a) ☐ You think 'How can that guy afford a dog? There's no way you'd give him anything.

    b) ☐ You'd give clothes or food but money might be spent on booze or drugs. Anyway, sometimes these people follow you, if you're too generous.

    c) ☐ You'd give if you could afford to. What he does with his money and life is his affair.

6. **You return, tired, from a trip to find that someone has parked in front of your house. So you:**

    a) ☐ Double park, to block in the offender and when they knock on your door give them some icy sarcasm.

    b) ☐ Realising this must be a friend of your neighbours' you make a mental note to do the same thing to them next time they are away.

♏ SCORPIO ♏

c) ☐ Seeing the notice stuck in your neighbours' window you realise that they must all be up the road organising a charity jumble sale. You park up the road and go to the church hall for a coffee and a chat.

7. **Your partner gives you a mobile telephone for Christmas. Some say it's the modern equivalent of a chastity belt – but who's wearing it?**

    a) ☐ You wonder why your partner gave it to you. Was it to convince you that he or she is faithful at all times, when that isn't the case?

    b) ☐ It will be useful in all sorts of ways to check up on things in advance. When you aren't calling out you'll keep it switched off, so no one can get hold of you.

    c) ☐ It was a kind and generous thought, but you won't use it often because you usually know what you need to know.

8. **Your crowd at the pub is talking about sex and gender differences. It's the sort of topic that keeps going because everyone finds it fascinating. Do you join in?**

    a) ☐ This is a great opportunity to find out just what everyone thinks so you listen carefully. Who knows when it might come in handy.

    b) ☐ You smile enigmatically, and when asked your views you mouth a platitude. You aren't going to let anyone close on that subject.

    c) ☐ You deepen the tone by saying something like 'The mind is the most erogenous zone' and see what happens.

9. **Someone in your circle of acquaintances has recently suffered a bereavement. How do you react?**

    a) ☐ You take the opportunity to talk to him or her when you can, to find out the details of the fatal illness.

Introduction

b) ☐ You keep away from the bereaved because you feel privacy should be respected at this time.

c) ☐ You realise how the bereaved must be feeling and you quietly offer to help in any way you can, should he or she wish it.

Now count up your score. What do you have most of – a's, b's or c's?

Mostly a's. It seems that you are the 'paranoid' type of Scorpio. Of course, this does not mean that you suffer from clinical paranoia, so perhaps 'suspicious' would be a better term – *very* suspicious, and sometimes vengeful. You like to get to the bottom of everything, keep your own counsel and have an arsenal full of information about everyone else. You know that knowledge is power, but do you really know how to use it? Perhaps you have been hurt at some time, but do you realise that your attitude to life is creating an environment where you are setting yourself up to be hurt again? Start to have a little trust in life and human nature and use your considerable powers of penetration in a more positive way that will create a better environment for yourself. Ever heard of positive thinking?

Mostly b's. You're the 'obscure' type of Scorpio. You are canny and sceptical. You like your privacy and you respect that of others, except when they infringe upon your rights. Then you are quite capable of holding a grudge. Your attitude can be a little negative – do you really need to protect yourself so closely? And wouldn't your creativity be better used making a more interesting and fulfilling life for yourself, rather than watching your back? Sometimes you cut off your nose to spite your face, perhaps without realising it. Forget that sting, stop lurking behind rocks – make like an eagle and soar.

SCORPIO

Mostly c's. You don't need much advice from me or anyone else about how to use your powers of penetration and intuition. You have the confidence to take care of others and you are probably excellent at it. You are courageous, curious, realistic, and – yes – powerful. You know how to be who you are and let others also be themselves. Some people are bound to be a little afraid of you, but that's their problem, I guess. Remember that not everyone is happy to be seen through or confronted, so be gentle!

If you found that in many cases none of the answers seemed anywhere near to fitting you then it may be that you are an uncharacteristic Scorpio. This may be because there are factors in your astrological chart that frustrate the expression of your Sun sign, or it may be because there is a preponderance of other signs, outweighing the Scorpio part. Whatever the case may be, your Sun-sign potential needs to be realised. Perhaps you will find something to ring a few bells in the following pages.

1 The essential Scorpio

I know the bottom, she says. I know it with my great tap root:
It is what you fear.
I do not fear it: I have been there . . .
I have suffered the atrocity of sunsets
Scorched to the root . . .
Now I break up in pieces that fly about like clubs.
A wind of such violence
Will tolerate no bystanding: . . .

Sylvia Plath, 'Elm (for Ruth Fainlight)'

■ THE POWER AND THE PASSION

Many people are a little afraid of Scorpio – and that sometimes includes the Scorpions themselves! A smattering of astrological knowledge defines Scorpio as megalomaniac, sex maniac and paranoid, and if that isn't enough to put each and every Scorpio behind bars, you can add vengeful, devious, cruel and malicious to the list. Need I go on? Scorpio readers will not shrivel – they have more guts than that. It is true that most Scorpios are strong-willed, intense and very private people. However, this sign is the most maligned.

Most Scorpios present a bland and innocent exterior. Well, they would, wouldn't they? And yet that isn't so very misleading, for while no Scorpio alive is ever truly bland, this is a deeply compassionate and exquisitely sensitive sign. There, Scorpio's best-kept secret is out already. Can you wonder you are 'paranoid' at times?

SCORPIO BODY LANGUAGE

Scorpio movements are usually smooth and often quite unobtrusive. You sometimes seem to have the gift of invisibility – if you don't want to be noticed often you aren't, and this gives you more chance to observe. Other members of your sign have a dramatic, charismatic persona that it is hard to miss a mile off. More generally, Scorpios belie all the propaganda by being pleasant and quite 'average' in most respects. You are good at camouflage. There is often a slow and fairly deliberate air and usually Scorpios do not spread themselves, preferring to keep arms, legs, briefcase and handbag quite close to the body. When the occasion calls for it you are usually mistress or master of the meaningful glance, conveying a hypnotic allure if you so choose or exuding psychic prickles to keep off the unwanted. Members of this sign do sometimes seem to see very deeply into others and have a habit of answering unasked questions.

MYTHS OF THE SCORPION

The most common myth about the Scorpio constellation is that the gods sent this beast to attack the hunter Orion, who had become conceited and challenged their power (this is one of the myths about the death of Orion). Yet another story concerns Phaëthon, son of Helios the Sun-god, who boasted that he could drive the chariot of the Sun, but a scorpion came and stung the ankles of the wild steeds, who bolted, and Phaëthon was flung to his death.

In both of these cases the scorpion punished hubris – a vaunting pride that over-reached itself. Pride is certainly a Scorpio motif, and people may say, along with Milton's Lucifer 'Better to reign in Hell that serve in Heaven'. However, Scorpio is equally linked to death and transformation, and members of the sign will sometimes put themselves in the path of inevitable destruction, in order to force themselves into a transition.

♏ The essential Scorpio ♏

The scorpion is an interesting animal that is capable of stinging itself to death if surrounded by overwhelming odds – and if you are a true Scorpio you would far rather self-destruct than yield and lose control over your own destiny. Scorpions are not insects, for they belong to the same family as spiders, the Arachnida. They have pincer claws to seize their prey and a sting in the tail, which, in some species, is very dangerous. Scorpions inhabit the warm parts of the globe and are nocturnal, emerging at night to hunt and mate. They have enormous stamina and have been known to survive in the vicinity of nuclear test. The young cling to their mother's back for several days after birth, feeding by osmosis off her intestinal juices. All these characteristics are often evident in Scorpio – strength, survival instinct, stealth, and ability to give themselves at the deepest level, as the mother scorpion to her offspring.

> **In Egyptian mythology Selket is the scorpion goddess. Scorpions stung Horus, son of Isis, but the other scorpions saved him, and attacked a boy whose mother had refused to help, in revenge. Isis then, in turn, saved that boy, through her magic. Selket was a friend of Isis, wearing her horns and Sun disk on her head. She symbolises resurrection into the new life that follows earthly existence, and she forms a connection, helping the newly dead to grow accustomed to their changed existence. One of her tasks was to guard the Canopic jars, which held, among other things, the intestines of the deceased, so forming a link with the feeding of the young scorpions.**

These funereal themes are Scorpionic, for the sign is connected with death and all that is hidden, and indeed sacred. However, if all this seems too sepulchral, remember that Selket was a goddess of awesome and ethereal beauty. In Scorpio we find a connection with the dark face of the ancient Great Mother Goddess. Terrifying she may be, but all her initiates are aware that by facing her appalling countenance and embracing her hackles, she then reveals herself as beautiful, gentle and offering passage into new life.

♏ SCORPIO ♏

■ ELEMENT, QUALITY AND RULING PLANET

We have seen that each of the signs of the zodiac belongs to one of the Elements, Earth, Fire, Air or Water, and one of the Qualities, Cardinal, Fixed or Mutable. Scorpio is Fixed Water. This means that Scorpio is deep and emotional. In some ways the idea of fixity in regard to the fluidity of water spells a contradiction, and it is true that Scorpio can be somewhat torn between extreme stubbornness and an osmotic awareness of the feelings and needs of others. All those born with an emphasis in the Water signs have strong emotions, responding with empathy and sympathy and having a profound knowledge of what goes on beneath the surface of both themselves and their companions. Human relationships are their motivating factor, and while Scorpio may sometimes seem bent on control and oneupmanship, they have an intense and occasionally almost desperate need for intimacy driving them to extremes.

We have also seen that the Element Water has some things in common with what Jung called the Feeling function. It is important to remember that 'feeling' here is not about emotions spilling everywhere in a gooey self-indulgence. Feeling people are often well in-tune with emotions, it is true, and because of this are often more able to control and conceal when necessary, and Scorpio is past master at this! True 'feeling' is about evaluating in human, social terms and about esteeming the bonds of love, family and friendship. In many ways this is what makes us warm human beings, and while it may not always be logical, Jung was quite clear that 'feeling' is a rational function, with its own systems of balance, sense and harmony. While many Scorpios show themselves to have active and extremely incisive minds, a predominance of Scorpio usually manifests itself in a powerful 'feeling' element. Scorpios often know exactly how other people are feeling and what they are thinking.

The essential Scorpio

Scorpio is the eighth sign of the zodiac and the second of the Water triad. Fiery Aries, the Pioneer, begins the cycle, followed by Earthy Taurus, the Farmer and Settler. Then we have Airy Gemini, the Communicator and Thinker, with Cancer, sign of the Family and the Clan, ushering us into experience of human bonds and developing society. After Cancer comes Leo, sign of the Monarch, and then Virgo, Sower of Seeds, Reaper and Pragmatic Analyst. The seventh sign is Airy Libra, sign of Partnership and Balance, bringing us up to date with Scorpio, penetrative sign of the Hidden, the Fundamental and the Transformative. Here we have a metaphor for human society and psyche, and while we all have each of the signs in our make-up, in some people certain signs are more marked. As we travel through the zodiac the signs become progressively more complex, and Scorpio is certainly the most complicated sign yet encountered.

In the Northern Hemisphere, Scorpio marks the time of year when life recedes from the surface and goes beneath the soil, to incubate in secret while darkness claims the land. The feast of Hallowe'en, also called by its more ancient name of Samhain, occurs when the Sun is in Scorpio. This is the festival of the ancestors, a time of nostalgia and withdrawal. In days gone by it marked a time of real loss, as livestock was sorted for slaughter and oncoming harshness of winter portended the death of the old and sickly. However, to the Celts, this was the New Year; to them all began in darkness. So day began at nightfall and the year began in autumn. Implicit in this is an honouring of the shadowed and repressed. Scorpionic motifs are recognisable here!

While in the north we prepare for the retreat and privacy of winter, in the Southern Hemisphere all is thrusting, vibrant growth as spring really gets under way. This can be seen as the sexual, powerful and life-affirming aspect of Scorpio, promising regeneration and rebirth and showing, with all the drama of which nature is capable, that life is there to be enjoyed.

♏ SCORPIO ♏

Each sign is said to have a 'Ruling Planet'. This means that there is a planet that has a special affinity with the sign, whose energies are most at home when expressed in terms of that sign. The Ruling Planet for Scorpio is Pluto, since its discovery earlier in the century. Formerly the honour went to Mars, and Scorpio was called its 'night house', displaying its worst characteristics with medieval malevolence. We are now wiser about Scorpio, and Pluto, Lord of the Underworld, is a more fitting ruler, although the fighting spirit of Scorpio can be laudably martial, especially in protection of others.

Pluto and Persephone

The story of the abduction of Persephone by Pluto is well known. Persephone is a nymph, daughter of the nature goddess Demeter, and when she seeks to pluck a unique and glorious flower the earth opens, and lo and behold, there rises up Pluto in his black chariot. He seizes the maiden and takes her with him down into his dark kingdom. Meanwhile Demeter searches for her daughter, calling desperately. She withdraws her protection from the land and the first winter stalks a countryside that is now harsh and frozen. The gods arrange that Persephone shall return to her mother if she has eaten nothing while in the kingdom of Hades, but she has nibbled a pomegranate, and so she must spend part of the year in the dark realms, reigning as Queen of the Underworld and returning to her mother for six months of the year (some versions say eight). In this way the cycle of the seasons is determined, for Demeter blesses the land with summer while her daughter is with her and withdraws, leaving all in winter's claws, when Persephone leaves.

The idea of cyclicity and the inevitability of fate is well known to Scorpio. All that is born dies, all that dies shall be reborn – thus says the tale of Demeter, Persephone and Pluto. Looking deeper at the myth we see that this is also an initiation tale. Pluto initiates

Persephone into her sexuality: he is emissary of the Dark Mother – I do not think we visualise Persephone struggling against Pluto's embrace. The pomegranate, which seals her fate, is a symbol of fertility. The joy of sex, as well as its ability to transform us and reveal to us parts of ourselves we had not acknowledged, themes of loss, of cyclicity, of redemption and fertility – all these are Scorpionic matters. Scorpio will go where others fear to tread. Of course, these are extreme matters, rarely apparent in the daily round. Suffice to say that Scorpios know a thing or two and are rarely deceived by appearances.

MAGICIANS AND SEX MANIACS

Scorpios are often interested in aspects of the occult, in psychotherapy or in subjects on the fringes of established science. You are natural sleuths, uncovering other people's best-kept secrets and knowing just where the cupboard is that contains the cobwebby skeleton. You can usually pinpoint areas of vulnerability, too. Add to this a certain secrecy about your own personal affairs and an enigmatic air, and you have a perfect screen on which people can project their own fears. A Scorpio who keeps apart, feeling that their realms of experience are outside the orbit of more mundane individuals, or feeling there really is something to hide, is a magnet for all repressed anxieties. Such a Scorpio may make people uneasy – here we have all that is 'forbidden'. What might this person be capable of? Best give Scorpio a wide berth.

We need to unpack these notions, for they are largely unfounded. Scorpios are human, like everyone else. They have no 'special powers'. Most are pleasant individuals concealing nothing more nefarious than their own vulnerability. Whence comes the 'magical' aura that we associate with the Scorpion?

SCORPIO

The truth lies in a transformative quality that is associated with the sign, and which is within the reach of all strongly Plutonic individuals. Of course, many Scorpios choose not to connect with this aspect of themselves. Self-protective and often secretive, sometimes resentful, often desirous, with a sense of walking, perhaps, in the shadow of the hand of fate, they pursue a mundane existence. However, another symbol often allied to Scorpio is that of the phoenix – magical bird that rises reborn from the flames of its own funeral pyre. Scorpios who are the 'phoenix' type are prepared to face the flames of their own inner self, of all that is fearful or denied and to live through this. They do not shun extreme experience, because they know there lies a truth and a reality. They may brave destruction in their own lives, or face the unnameable on behalf of others, such as in working with the dying or bereaved. In such a way Scorpio can bring out into daylight that which is most terrifying and transform it into something that will bestow new life, or usher in a fresh phase of existence.

One of the most transformative experiences available to us is that of sexual union with another person. Sex, for Scorpio is a matter of the soul and the spirit, and while ecstacy is achieved through bodily means, it is not mere physical gratification that is sought. In a way Scorpio seeks to escape the bounds of earthy existence, not by denying or 'rising above' but by finding the eternal in the here and now, by the glory of the passions. Of course, not all sexual experience is that intense or transfiguring, and Scorpio may be well aware that one has to kiss a lot of frogs before one finds a prince! This sign is one of the most realistic when it comes to distinguishing between what is just 'good sex' and what is real love. Of course, sex is power and Scorpio is not blind to the advantages of this, but the reputation the sign has for indiscriminate seduction and promiscuity is largely exaggerated.

■ OLD LASER-EYES

Much is made of the 'penetrating Scorpio stare' – but perhaps too much emphasis has been placed on this, both in those with Scorpio as a Rising or Sun sign. After all, a penetrating stare is a dead give-away, and any Scorpio knows that you find out less if your probings are obvious. 'Come to bed eyes' are another matter, and Plutonic individuals can have a most hypnotic and seductive look that penetrates down into your very soul, if they so choose. Certainly Scorpio is deep-seeing, spotting hypocrisy and insincerity at a hundred paces. These are not easy people to fool.

However, there is much more to Scorpionic penetration than a determination to get to the bottom of everything and everyone. Yes, Scorpio may do this, in the belief that knowledge is power. Often it is true that Scorpio cannot help knowing how other people feel, because like all the Water signs you soak up atmospheres like a sponge. Because of this you need methods of self-protection, and this makes certain Scorpios loners or causes them to emit an enigmatic smokescreen. You are susceptible to the pain of others because you are profoundly sensitive and very easily hurt yourselves by criticism, rejection or a lack of loving intensity – a fact which is often missed in descriptions of Scorpio. You will move in a variety of ways to protect yourselves, but you are extremely empathic and caring people who will often move heaven and Earth to help a friend, and who can be gentle, compassionate, understanding and fiercely protective. The laser cuts both ways. Scorpio not only penetrates, but is penetrated, and the pain so experienced is often what spurs Scorpio to tackle situations others would shun, because 'someone has to do it'.

♏ SCORPIO ♏

■ THE WORM IN THE APPLE

Ironically, the faults of this mysterious sign are the most well-publicised and the most obvious in the zodiac: suspicion, jealousy and hunger for power. Because you are so intensely aware of your own vulnerability, attack often seems the best form of defence, and you are certainly capable of manoeuvring yourselves into a position of superiority and control in the most devious fashion. This may be easier to forgive if we remember that the reason for this is a most vivid sense of one's own sensitivity to hurt. One of Scorpio's principal motives is often self-defence.

However, knowledge of the 'darker' side of life may make it impossible for Scorpio to trust. If you are constantly subject to a kind of psychic bombardment in the shape of the repressed desires, fantasies and aggressive urges of those around you, if you are always aware of hidden motives and that things are *never* what they seem, then you may just become so suspicious that you are never able to take anything at face value, and will see the corrupt even where, for once, all is innocence. Scorpio may not be able to recognise what is obvious – the good intentions and affection of others, and simple enjoyment. To stretch the analogy of the worm in the apple, you may be so sure that something revolting lurks in each rosy fruit that the kitchen may be littered with pulp and peel before you are convinced. It is not easy, but every Scorpio does need to make an effort to believe and hope, for these are creative acts and may generate the very reality that is desired – we all blossom in the ray of confidence and trust.

We do also encounter the 'textbook' type of Scorpio – the sort who believes their own myth and comes out with phrases like 'I'll get him' – believe me, I have heard these very words. They are un-Scorpionic because they are so obvious, and all such a one 'gets' is a life of isolation. A Scorpio who is really powerful knows that true power is 'power to' not 'power over' – they are never obvious and malicious only on very, very rare occasions. Then offenders can be sure they deserve it and they'd better head for a fallout shelter.

Along with the other Water signs, Scorpio may share a tendency for opinions to be emotionally based, and therefore unreasonable and unmodified by detached thought. Besides, the observant side to Scorpio can show as criticism and pernicketiness. Add to this a few hard knocks and a propensity for seeing mostly that which is undesirable and concealed, and there is a recipe for some very rigid and negative attitudes, such as 'All men are bastards' or 'All women are out for what they can get'. This can wreak havoc in lives and is a self-fulfilling prophecy. After all, if you continually disbelieve and punish your partner he may behave like a 'bastard', and if you relentlessly deprive the woman you love of what she needs she is bound to come over as grasping – and you will soon find yourself alone. We are confronted by the need to trust again, and also by the need to develop an open mind. Scorpios need to remind themselves of what they know – that human nature is infinitely varied and subtle – to save themselves from being imprisoned by stereotypes.

NOTHING IN MODERATION

This sign is not comfortable with temperance and restraint, for you sense that it is not real, not about what truly throbs and burns beneath the skin and within the soul. Encounters with others have to be profound and meaningful – and here Scorpio may be caught in something of a dilemma, for such encounters require that one makes oneself vulnerable. You may resolve this by trying to control the one you love, sometimes virtually by house arrest, so that where you have 'garnered up your heart' is safely under lock and key. Because of this Scorpio, sign of unbridled passion, can also be known as a control freak.

♏ SCORPIO ♏

This can mean a contradiction that strangles Scorpio, for in the end no true transcendence or transformation is found in a locked vault. You need to summon all your considerable guts in order to allow yourselves to be vulnerable. Openness to pain is the price for peak experience, and no one knows better than Scorpio that all things have a price. However, as your self-awareness and belief grows, along with it comes the knowledge that self-protection is always possible, and that control and retaliation are as unnecessary as they are unproductive. Wise Scorpio knows that while human beings are always frail, the universe can be trusted.

The Frog and the Scorpion

Once there was a frog and a scorpion on the river bank. 'I want to get to the other side,' said the scorpion. 'Will you take me on your back?'

The frog, backing off, but trying not to look too obvious, said 'I don't know about that. After all, you might sting me.'

'Oh, come now,' responded the scorpion. 'If I were to sting you, you would sink and die and then I too would drown.'

Feeling that to refuse would seem foolish and unreasonable, the frog reluctantly agreed and the scorpion crawled aboard his back.

Into the water jumped the frog and paddled energetically for the opposite bank. But when they were halfway across, the scorpion stung him in the back of the neck. As he felt the deadly poison course through him, he cried out with his last gasp 'Why?'

'Because I felt like it,' answered the scorpion, as the waves closed over both of them.

This can be taken as a cautionary tale on the theme 'never trust a Scorpio'. However, it is a rare Scorpio who enacts something so

♏ The essential Scorpio ♏

utterly and meaninglessly self-destructive. Really this story is about how Scorpio views life – it is best to act as if everyone can be so illogically, unpredictably and self-destructively vicious as the scorpion in the story. It isn't so much that the scorpion epitomises Scorpio, as that Scorpio would *never* be like the frog – afraid to trust his or her own instincts, unnecessarily being exposed to risk, for neither love nor any other advantage, just because it seemed 'reasonable'. Wise Scorpio knows that life is not 'reasonable' – it's not a bad way to be.

■ PRACTICE AND CHANGE ■

- Never be 'caught by your own myth'. You are only vengeful, devious and controlling if you choose to be.
- Do not be tempted to hold yourself aloof and alone. Learn also to appreciate those who live life on the surface. Take their simple way of relating and giving affection at face value.
- Your feelings are deeply intuitive. Do not attempt to crystallise them into dogma or stereotypes.
- Remember that you have a talent for self-transformation and you can cope with just about anything. Know deep inside that you can remake yourself whatever the situation.
- Lack of trust is a self-fulfilling prophecy – don't get caught in it.
- Do let others teach you to open out. You aren't the only sensitive soul in the world.
- Your ability to see below the surface is a gift – do not let it become a trap. Your job is to redeem and make available.
- Let your knowledge empower you, not depress you. Look for the beautiful and the true, and it will become part of you.

2 ♏ Relationships

. . . look for me by moonlight,
Watch for me by moonlight,
I'll come to thee by moonlight, though hell should bar the way

Alfred Noyes, 'The Highwayman'

. . . I had rather be a toad,
And live upon the vapour of a dungeon
Than keep a corner in the thing I love
For others' use

Shakespeare, *Othello*

Nothing unites, body, soul and spirit as powerful sexual experience is capable of doing. And no one is more able to appreciate this than those in whom the sign Scorpio is strong. However, you are vividly aware of the raw, physical aspect of sexual union. Some Scorpios are torn ragged on the dilemma of body and spirit, while others see that physical pleasure is a divine gift and a potent means to union and transcendence. Whatever the case, nothing with you is ever simple, and to assign you the role of sex machine is most misleading. Despite your reputation, it is rare for you to take pleasure where you find it, like bees among the honeysuckle. Usually matters are too highly charged for this. You are aware of the undercurrents at play in every human encounter and issues of control and manipulation, as well as surrender and ecstasy, are always a reality for you. You can behave in a promiscuous or unscrupulous manner: you may exhibit a cynical sensuality, but you may also choose a life of celibacy and explicit spirituality rather than trust yourselves on the storm-tossed waters of human interaction. Occasionally you can become prudish and fanatical about sex, evangelising about moral decline, but it is always a shame when you do this, for it means repression and denial in a sign that is usually so courageous. At your best, no one is more capable than you of understanding the nuances, the poignancy, the compulsion, the tragedy and the sublimity of sexual relationships.

Much is made of the suspicious and jealous side of Scorpio, and this often is a fact. Where Scorpio loves, there you want everything. This is because you give so very much and are so exquisitely sensitive and profoundly passionate. Only total security and commitment will give you peace of mind – however, Scorpio is not obviously 'tropical'. Self-control and detachment are much more in evidence.

Scorpio encounters are very rarely superficial. Like kamikaze pilots, you sometimes seem bent on destruction in the flames of your own desires. Sometimes you may become cynical and sceptical; at others you may brood on the 'one that got away'. Scorpios are often tempted to try to remake their partners, partly to control them and partly because this sign of transformation is alive to the potentials in everyone. Whether others emerge from it bruised and bleeding or lifted to another dimension, they won't forget their encounter with Scorpio!

SCORPIO SEXUALITY

Scorpio can be a fantastic lover. Scorpio is the sign of erotica – that outward manifestation of human arousal and response – and a vast spectrum of experience comes under your domain. You are capable of a finely modulated, almost psychic attunement to your lover while at the same time drawing on the wellsprings of your own passion. Scorpio has a certain magic and a hotline to that quivering, exquisitely vulnerable part of the human being that trembles between life and death, animal and divine, agony and ecstacy. However, Scorpio's paramount concern is the emotions, not the paltry fizzle of bodily satisfaction.

There are a few more considerations to be borne in mind. For one thing, Scorpio has a long fuse when it comes to sexual response – you rarely fling off your clothes and pounce, and you are far too proud and alive to the responses of others to force an issue. You will often keep your passions on a choke lead, fearing vulnerability. Most Scorpios expect a lot and are very choosy about where they park their love-wagon. Some, in fact, are so uptight that fear of 'letting go' may deny them the release which they crave. Such Scorpios may be cold and withdrawn.

Power is sometimes a motivation in sexual encounters, and sex can be used as a weapon by Scorpio, used to tantalise or enslave, or withheld as a punishment. Because of this, Scorpio has been called cruel, although this is usually unjust. At the risk of repeating myself, this is a sensitive sign and ploys are motivated by self-protection.

Female Scorpio

Scorpio women appreciate erotic ambience and long drawn-out encounters that allow the intoxication of intimacy to permeate every corner. Expressions of feeling and romance are very important to them. Yes, they do pick up on the wordless, but nonetheless words of love can be very arousing. Some Scorpio ladies present a mouseish exterior, reluctant to advertise their sexuality or to be obtrusive. Others exude sensual power in their appearance, sometimes explicitly seductive in true vamp style. To some men they can be irresistibly hypnotic, to others quite hostile. Ms Scorpio guards her autonomy – usually this is a lady who knows her own mind. She is no one's simpering darling, but a tigress with claws – fierce and exciting. Yes, she can be a deliciously feminine pussy-cat, or she can be repressed by guilt, but she is never a pushover. Her reputation as one of the most seductive ladies in the zodiac is deserved.

Male Scorpio

With Mr Scorpio there is no more Mr Nice Guy. The Scorpio male believes that only losers play for the sake of the game. Scorpio plays to win and he will rarely show his hand until sure of the prize. He is more capable of turning his emotions off than his female counterpart and can be coldly sensual on occasion. Scorpio will often seem boyish or quite ordinary, but he has an enigmatic quality and a magnetic core. He is usually much more controlled than the Scorpio female, and I have heard Scorpio men extol the virtues of keeping emotions on a tight rein. Scorpio doesn't deny – he usually has a pretty good idea of who and where his demons are, and he binds them with a tight cord – until, one dark night, they break free and drag him somewhere wild and dark. From that encounter he emerges refined and newly smelted into a finer human being, or even more hell bent on steely control.

The wishes of Savitri

Savitri was an Indian princess, and when her father exorted her to marry, she insisted she wished to travel the land in disguise, to see whom fate brought her way. At length she met a handsome man called Satyavan, whose father was a dispossessed and blinded king. They fell in love and promised faith to each other.

When Savitri returned to her father's castle and announced her intention, everyone turned pale, for a holy man revealed that Satyavan was under a curse and would die in twelve months. However, with a sad heart Savitri clung to her promise. She married her love and went to live with him in poverty.

One day as they were walking, Satyavan fell, clutching his head, and lay still on a carpet of leaves. Savitri ran to him, but the god Yama stood before her with a noose in his hand. 'Weep not,' said he, 'all Satyavan's sorrows are now over.'

♏ SCORPIO ♏

He placed his rope around Satyavan's neck and his soul separated and walked away with Yama. Savitri followed. Turning to look at her, Yama's eyes flamed.

'So, you would follow the god of death?' said Yama. 'Very well, you shall have one wish – anything except the life of your husband.'

'Then let my father-in-law's sight be restored,' said Savitri.

'It is done,' replied Yama. 'Farewell.'

But Savitri still followed to where the forest grew dense and dark. At length Yama turned. He seemed to have grown in stature and his shadow stretched black into the undergrowth. 'So, still you come behind me,' he said. 'Very well, girl, you shall have one more wish. Then cease this folly.'

'I choose that my father-in-law's kingdom be restored,' replied Savitri.

'So be it,' decreed Yama, and still holding the rope that bound her beloved, he turned and moved on. But Savitri continued to follow though the noxious breath of the forest choked her. More dead than alive she stumbled amid thorns and brambles, always following the footsteps of the grim pair ahead.

Once more Yama turned, and now he seemed as tall as an elm and his voice sounded like the rush of a tempest in the tree-tops. 'Still you follow, foolish girl,' he cried. 'I could destroy you. Yet you have the strength and courage of ten men. One last wish will I grant, and this time let it be something for yourself.'

'Just one thing do I want,' she responded. 'Let me have many children and live to see my grandchildren grow in strength and happiness.'

> 'It shall be,' said Yama, and his breath sighed on the troubled air.
>
> 'But you forget,' said Savitri, quietly, 'I am a Hindu, and according to our law a widow cannot remarry.'
>
> Silence spread over the forest as if all the dank life therein held its breath. If Savitri could not remarry, how could Yama keep his word, except ... Suddenly, the laughter of the god of death rang out over the leaping shadows.
>
> 'Well done, well done, my courageous and cunning daughter,' cried Yama. Releasing the noose from Satyavan's neck he returned her husband to her. 'You shall have back the only man who can father your children,' he said. 'Farewell – it will be many years before we shall meet again.'

This story of intense love, courage and commitment even in the jaws of death, tells us much about the strength of true passion in the sign of Scorpio. Sometimes it does seem as if Scorpio has to go through hell itself to attain what is desired, but the rewards are shown to be worth it.

SCORPIO WOMAN IN LOVE

Ms Scorpio demands a great deal in terms of commitment and loyalty. This she will reward with all the intense feeling and utter commitment of which she is capable. Failure she will punish resourcefully and relentlessly by withholding and manipulating. She is not a mate for the faint-hearted, but she is a gloriously fulfilling companion to any man who demands more than the superficial and is bored by sugary acquiescence. Ms Scorpio is not sweet – she is fathomless and she is capable of rewarding trust.

♏ SCORPIO ♏

The Scorpio female may do her share of bed-hopping in youth because she wants to experiment and explore the parameters of human experience. In the end, however, her emotional nature is best satisfied by a single meaningful and intense partnership which gives her the opportunity to scale heights and scour depths that are unavailable in casual encounters. This is not a woman who will drop her guard – or anything else – very easily. She needs to be wooed and she needs to trust. Then slowly she opens out and blossoms. Ms Scorpio needs to know where she stands and she will not step on uncertain ground.

Although Scorpio ladies will be unfaithful if frustrated or emotionally denied, they rarely do this without guilty torments. Yes, they can be devious, and if Ms Scorpio wants to hide something rest assured it will stay hidden until the crack of doom. However, infidelity violates Ms Scorpio's notion of how love should be – this is not an ideal or dream but a knowledge that she can never find what she seeks in this way, and is in fact betraying herself. Ms Scorpio would far, far rather unfold her secrets in a single, secure relationship.

To this woman sex can be a matter of devastating ecstasy or something faintly disgusting if not conducted with due sensitivity and passionate immersion. Unless Ms Scorpio is totally secure, she may have trouble really letting go, sexually, and she protects herself with as many provisos as possible. Despite her propensity for total abandonment, Ms Scorpio will usually need to hang on to some autonomy in a relationship and this may well entail having her own money supply or property. Also, for Ms Scorpio, times of intimacy need to be balanced by times when she has her own space – a secure Scorpio is not invasive, but respects her own independence and that of others.

A man looking for a life of domestic bliss with a dimpled innocent or who wants someone you can dominate or deceive, should look elsewhere – this is not your woman. If, however, he wants a life of excitement and fervency with someone who is half-angel, half-devil, and prepared to travel uncharted territories of the soul, then he should take the hand of Ms Scorpio. Sometimes he will be in heaven, sometimes in hell, but he will always know he's alive!

SCORPIO MAN IN LOVE

This man is every bit as intense and sensitive as his female counterpart, but conventions being what they are, he conceals the sensitivity more ruthlessly than she does, and often expresses the intensity as determination, detachment and conquest. It is true that he can play macho-man. He may have the old double standard down to a fine art, justifying it on the basis of the differing needs of men and women, but make no mistake – it's *his* needs he's really talking about. If he loves, then he is utterly, mind-blowingly committed and terribly vulnerable. Can you blame him if he tries to fit his lover with ball, chain and chastity belt, while trying to maintain his own freedom? The fact is, he's not free and never will be, and you can see the truth of this in his eyes.

Cruelty is not a Scorpionic monopoly, but this sign can sometimes enjoy inflicting emotional and physical pain, and this can be translated to sadistic sex, on very rare occasions. While this is really unforgivable, it stems from a fear of and a need for a searing intimacy that is at once the deepest desire and the greatest threat. There has also to be respect, gentleness, caring, mutual support and practical help. Without this, Mr Scorpio is in danger of destroying all he holds dear and remaining embittered among the wreckage feeling that no one has ever loved him enough. They may have – it's just that the armour plating wore a bit thin and they have gone off to find something that wasn't a battle-ground. Mr Scorpio may look a gift horse in the mouth once too often, until it bolts and all that's left is the taste of dust in his mouth.

At his best, however, this man is capable of an almost telepathic empathy, and of giving his heart and soul while retaining his critical faculties. When he says 'forever' he means it – not just 'until death do us part'. His sexuality has the power of a tidal wave and the subtlety of a veiled glance. In addition, he is deeply compassionate and protective of those he loves to the very death. What he wants is response, not submission, and he will probably respect his lover if she gives him a good fight sometimes. The true Scorpio man in love is incapable of betrayal. He is dependable, supportive, possessive and dominating, like the best romantic heroes, and he respects those who respect themselves. A woman who prefers something more bland should look elsewhere. However, if she prizes intensity, this guy will never be lukewarm or boring. She should think before she commits herself – the Scorpio arms will never let her go.

GAY SCORPIO

Sexual expression is overwhelmingly important to this sign, and while some Scorpios may decide to be celibate through guilt or fear of ostracism, they are never happy with this. Intimate contact with another human being is something for which Scorpio can become quite desperate, and gay Scorpios who, for some reason, feel they cannot 'come out' or form relationships that are meaningful to them, can be among the most unhappy of people.

Gay Scorpios really must find a way of coming to terms with themselves – really, this won't just 'go away' and while you may be able to hide perfectly how you feel, you cannot deceive yourself into believing you are fulfilled. You need to talk, and give yourself permission to enjoy sex in the way you prefer. It is your way to the realms of the spirit.

Some Scorpios, on the other hand, are quite open about their sexual feelings, and rightly so. Of course, no one – certainly not Scorpio – reveals all their secrets, but there can be a courage and commitment about this sign that makes other people brave, too. Scorpios can be trailblazers when it comes to sexual matters of all kinds – Freud had Scorpio rising. We all have a right to be happy and fulfilled in the type of human love we need.

SCORPIO LOVE TRAPS

The Wrecker

We have spoken of Scorpionic power hunger, but the Wrecker is power ravenous. Again, the motivation is a deep vulnerability. By seduction, drama and disaster the Wrecker proves that he or she can rouse emotions and disrupt lives. There can be a real kick out of luring the happily married into betrayal and debauchery, and of intruding upon the happiness of others, hauling what has been relegated to the shadows out into the red light of forbidden sexual encounter. When feelings aroused for him or her have been strong enough to ruin someone's life and contentment, then this person feels powerful and desired – but never feels loved because he or she is not lovable and the Wrecker leaves the scene, letting others pick up the pieces and find peace of mind again – something the Wrecker never finds. For a while the Wrecker may feel warm and good inside, but it never lasts and he or she looks for another scene to shred.

The Wrecker does provide one function, and that is to reveal what has been repressed. Hopefully this can be a positive function and personalities and partnerships can be remade in a position of greater awareness. However, for the Wrecker him or herself there is never going to be any lasting contentment unless something is faced. Manipulating people, playing with their emotions is a poor substitute for the real power, that is positive development of one's own potential. Unless the Wrecker can face up to his or her own neediness and longing for love; unless he or she achieves the maturity that perceives upsetting people is the work of a malevolent and lonely child, the Wrecker is doomed to a life of loneliness. If you recognise yourself here, in however diluted a form, ask yourself what you really want and what power you really seek. Is is not 'power to' that you want, not 'power over'? Do you not really want the courage to let others close and let yourself be needed? Drop the idea of conquest and let yourself warm to the idea of love.

The Nose Amputee

We are all familiar with the expression 'cutting off your nose to spite your face' and we have seen an example of this in Chapter 1, where the scorpion stings the frog and consigns them both to a watery grave. Some Scorpios are like that, in ways large and small. If they are hurt or betrayed in however paltry or accidental a fashion, they will exact reparation, even if doing so hurts them just as much as their lover. A small example of this could be the Scorpio woman who goes into a mood because her partner is late, and decides that she won't respond to him sexually later on, as a punishment. The truth of the matter is the poor guy really *was* working late at the office in order to pay for the extended mortgage he has taken out to please her. He is rewarded by doubt and the coming of another Ice Age. But she suffers too, for she is denying herself sexual fulfilment and depriving the relationship of love and warmth. If this happens too often then the ice caps cover everything.

If this is you, in however mild a form, then best to ease up. One of the most important lessons for Scorpio is that of verbalising feelings, and partners of Scorpios and the Scorpions themselves should be aware of this. Maybe you do feel hurt and suspicious – talk it through, don't punish yourself.

SCORPIO AND MARRIAGE

Many Scorpios delay or avoid marriage altogether because they are afraid of the commitment entailed or of relinquishing control over their lives to someone else. However, it is only in a committed and secure relationship – which is not necessarily a literal marriage, but amounts to the same thing – that you Scorpios can truly achieve the depth of contact you need. By loving intimacy you are able to know another person in all your varied expressions and levels, and that is the sort of encounter the Scorpion needs.

Once the vow is made, whatever form it takes, you take it very seriously indeed. Betrayal to you is a big word – you cannot flutter from blossom to blossom for sheer enjoyment. If you are betrayed yourself you will exact revenge in some form – you can take it as read. Even if you are one of the understanding, evolved types of Scorpio there is a savage justice about you that takes an eye for an eye, and even then you may not be able to reinstate the relationship on its former footing. If a partner has cheated on a Scorpio and been found out (which will probably be the case, unless the partner is *very* clever and watchful, with one eye open even in sleep) and if he or she then wants to retrieve the relationship, there is only one thing for it. The cheating partner should stand still, accept the retaliation and recrimination, grit his or her teeth and be prepared to stand there for a very long time, in extreme discomfort. Time and endurance may convince this Fixed sign that the partner really is sorry. The partner should give Scorpio the space to rant and rave, and try to talk and explain as much as possible, holding nothing back about deepest motivations. If he or she really loves Scorpio, in time Scorpio will come to know it too. Hang on!

Basically, Scorpio is 'the marrying kind' and makes a very dependable partner as long as certain safeguards are in place. These concern the autonomy we spoke of earlier. You will never relinquish control of your whole life to another person, unless for some reason you are punishing yourself with self-imposed martyrdom. You will always need to have areas that are not invaded, possessed or even visited by your nearest and dearest. Others should respect this, and hang on to a little independence, even if it is difficult at times.

■ WHEN LOVE WALKS OUT – HOW SCORPIO COPES

Scorpio may cope very well at the end of a love affair, for several reasons. One may be that you Scorpios, always cautious, have never opened the floodgates to your heart. Another may be that Scorpions, proud and secretive, would die rather than show they are hurt. A third may be the extreme stoicism of the sign, that really is able to grit its teeth and soldier on through a barren wasteland. A fourth reason may be the Scorpion's ability to make a complete transition, like the snake shedding its skin, or the phoenix from the flames, and leave the old life and love behind.

In youth Scorpio is often very dramatic, and so there may be lots of beginnings and endings. Maturity brings a different outlook. If this is a relationship that seemed '*la grande passion*', 'a forever kind of love', it is just possible that Scorpio will not be able to resort to any of the recovery strategies listed above, and that there is major breakdown, as if this is the end of the world. To Scorpio it feels that way. If this happens, then the 'breakdown' needs to run its course, and when the tears have stopped flowing, Scorpio will find a way to resurrect him or herself.

Yet another characteristic scenario – and perhaps the most dangerous – is the Scorpio who refuses to talk, or admit he or she is hurt and who behaves as if nothing has happened. This is different from pride or stoicism, although it may be hard to spot the distinction. This can be a Scorpio who is so scared of the intensity of feelings that he or she is 'into denial' and there may be at once a brittle feel and a disturbing emotional field. This sort of Scorpio *badly* needs to talk, either to friends and family, or if this is not possible then therapy really is a good idea, in order for the Scorpion to achieve the 'rebirth' of which the sign is capable. Until the relationship has been admitted to have died, and has been consciously mourned, no moving on is possible.

Starting afresh

The powerful emotions do need to be worked through and there may have to be a time when the Scorpion's life seems unmanageable to the point of falling apart, and while this may look alarming, these are people of extremes. Remember the phoenix? Great things can arise out of these flames, and will, in time. Sometimes the greater the conflagration, the more messy the wreckage the more complete the ensuing regeneration.

No one suffers more than Scorpio at the end of a relationship, for all the fixity of the sign is violated and the tremendously powerful emotions are in an agony. However, Scorpios truly are capable of pulling themselves up by their bootstraps, and will in time. Scorpio needs something to be passionate about – preferably not a new relationship too quickly. One thing to be wary of is that the Scorpion does not emerge only partly renewed carrying baggage of bitterness and cynicism. Nothing less than a reincarnation will do!

■ PRACTICE AND CHANGE ■

- Remember – you cannot remake others, it is futile, even destructive, to try. However, you can remake yourself – that is your talent. Always seek 'power to' never 'power over'.
- It is natural to want to control, in some form, anyone or anything that is deeply important to one's emotional well-being. However, you *can't*. Realising this will make your relationships more peaceful and pleasurable.
- An element of surrender is required to attain the intensity of experience you seek. Learn to develop a sense of trust in the universe and in your own ability to survive if things go wrong – it's worth the price.
- Jealousy may be your demon. Examine what in your past has contributed to these feelings and put the blame where it really belongs.
- If you use sex for power you pay a heavy price for a fleeting high – your own capacity for fulfilment. Ask yourself, is it worth it? Remember – 'power to' is the ideal.
- Do not settle for second best in relationships. Perfection is another matter, and very few of us find that. Look for the 'complete' rather than the 'perfect'.
- Verbalise your feelings. This may be one of the most difficult things you do, but give it your best shot.
- Remember that ordinary things like generosity, tenderness, support, affection and practical help are as important in relationships as passion.
- Make sure that any relationship allows you your own areas of autonomy.

3 All in the family

*Children aren't happy with nothing to ignore
And that's what parents were created for*

Ogden Nash, 'The Parent'

Usually a Scorpio in the family deepens the emotional tone. These people are aware of all the undercurrents and may react to them or play out other people's repressed feelings. Scorpio moods are sometimes a barometer of the family 'weather' and it is unfair to blame the Scorpio for being 'moody' when everyone else is festering in chagrin and wearing false smiles. It is very hard to have secrets with this person about, but to a family that offers Scorpio an emotional haven he or she is a source of strength and solace.

■ SCORPIO MOTHER

Scorpio mum is aware of the awesome responsibility she has undertaken. Not for her a sentimental world of pastel ribbons and talcum powder, or a chance to try out her pet psychological theories on a real, live guinea pig. She knows a human being is a complex and fateful creation and that all she does is important from her smiles and frowns to her choice of school. She feels it is her responsibility – if she is reasonably aware – not to pass on any family 'baggage' in the way of complexes and hang-ups. Add to this a wish to give the utmost care, the deepest love and the best training for life, and you have a gargantuan task on your hands. Small wonder that some Scorpios, harshly realistic about motherhood and its demands, decide to avoid the commitment and concentrate instead on other avenues of self-expression!

Those who choose motherhood bring to the role an unmatched dedication, bonding with their children at the most profound level. This is one of the most sensitive parents there are. She feels her children's hurts as her own, only magnified ten times, and will still be burning with mortification that several friends forgot her child's birthday party long after young Emma or Harry has dried the tears and got on with the serious business of enjoying themselves. She can be protective as a lioness, and may very occasionally be blind to her children's faults. However, she realises, as do all the Water signs, that fitting in with social mores is important, and generally her children's upbringing will reflect this.

Because this mum is about the wisest there is when it comes to humanity and its foibles, she may find it hard to let her children out of her sight, and this could make them nervous. Conversely, she has an extremely tough streak. She knows they have to learn to fight their own battles at some point, and one of her possible faults is that she may be 'cruel to be kind'. No one needs or deserves a break more than Scorpio mother, and she may realise that some separation is beneficial. One pitfall that Scorpio mum needs to avoid is that of withholding herself, in order to help her child come to terms with separation and to manage life in the big, bad world. She fears that too much reliance on her may make her child vulnerable. She needs the assurance that it is all right to give all her deepest love and attention, because a child who has their fill of this simply separates with relative ease, when the time is right.

On the other extreme, there are Scorpio mums who are very possessive and occasionally controlling. This sign is aware of the potential we all have, and will want to make the most of her child's abilities. This needs to be kept in check, or the children of Scorpio mum, will have no hope of deciding what to do, or be. Scorpio's talent is for spotting abilities – she should concentrate on providing an environment of opportunity, not pressure, and let nature do the rest.

If there are weaknesses in the child she will want to eradicate them, or at the very least give her best help so the child can overcome them. She may find it hard to accept imperfections because she fears the world will reject her child if it isn't capable in every sphere – not because she herself demands perfection for its own sake. Again, this mum needs to remind herself that the consciousness of her love is all the armour any child can need. Scorpio mother needs to show outward expressions of her love, for although her children are sure to sense her feelings – as children do – cuddles and closeness will give *her* pleasure.

No one is more capable than this mum of providing a child with a deep and abiding emotional security. She is wise and loving, a port in any storm and a source of advice, from all her rich experience, when problems arise.

■ SCORPIO FATHER

This man may expect high standards from his children and can appear stern, withdrawn, strict and cold. However, do not make the mistake of thinking this man is caught in a Victorian timewarp. He isn't into discipline for discipline's sake or espousing some antedeluvian moral code – he's into protection, in a big way. This means several things. First and foremost he wants to prepare his children for life, and no one knows better than he does how tough it is out there and how the pulse of the primitive beats beneath every polyester-clad chest. He also, like Scorpio mum, wants to protect his children from too great a dependence on his guardianship and generosity, and last but not least, if he is *very* honest with himself, he wants to protect himself from the vulnerability inflicted by his own emotions – because as soon as the wrinkled bundle is put into his arms he is enslaved for life, driven by a compulsion always to do the very best for this frail scrap of humanity. It's gruelling. Can you wonder that he puts up defences?

There is a gentle and humourous side to the Scorpio dad that emerges at times when he is relaxed and at peace. It is possible at such moments to spot the sensitive core that he hides so well. Scorpio dad does need to be very careful with the more sensitive children, whom he could possibly frighten, so hurting and distancing himself in the process – however, a true Scorpio, who has been tenderly treated himself, will always spot vulnerability and will be the first to coax out greater confidence in the gentlest, most subtle way. Scorpio can be his own worst enemy at times, distancing himself from his offspring because he fears too much closeness will result in vulnerability – but, of course, it won't. Like his female counterpart, the Scorpio father will protect at all costs. He is a champion that knows too well where all the dragon's lairs are to be found. Can you blame him if he acts tough at times?

THE SCORPIO CHILD

A Scorpio child is not the easiest to rear, but there are massive rewards. Never mind all the proud, tough, domineering, aggressive, stubborn tags; never mind all the stories about spider collections and a propensity for pulling the legs off flies. These are put about by people who do not understand Scorpio – and probably have never been close to one. (No Scorpio worth their salt would ever let anyone so obtuse close, in the first place!) Scorpio children are easier to rear, if you remember two things we have already stated about Scorpio – they are sensitive, and they need to conceal this fact.

♏ All in the family ♏

This isn't a child you can lie to. Most children see through lies to some extent, but to Scorpio they may be transparent as glass and Scorpio will be affronted and unsettled if you maintain the deception. They know what's in your handbag, your pocket, your mind and your heart, and furthermore they are capable of facing it, whatever it is. Don't patronise them or feel you have to protect them – the best protection is honesty. Scorpio can take most things from a very early age – except the withdrawal of love, that is.

It may seem that you need to be a cross between Mother Teresa and Freud to manage this child, but that is only because so many of us are emotionally dishonest and inhibited. With Scorpio you do need to accept that children are highly sexual beings, not the sugary cherubs of imagination. It also means that you need to understand sexuality – that it is a thing of the heart and mind as much as the body. Furthermore, childish sexuality, while it may be explicitly physical, is never the same as adult sexuality. Parents often become very worried about their children's developing sexuality, especially at adolescence. However, love, consideration and honesty is the formula for coping with all of this.

Young Scorpios may show earnest interest in their genitals (as indeed may any child) from a very early age. The Oedipal phase may be extra-intense with Scorpio, and they may seem obsessively devoted to the parent of the opposite sex from the time they are toddlers. This is where many parents, with the best of intentions, can slip up, rejecting the child for fear that something unhealthy is going on. It isn't. Of course, we all have to learn that we cannot marry our fathers or mothers and that fact, at some point in the process of maturing, can be very painful to accept. This pain can't be avoided, because it's life. However, the parent in question can show the utmost loving response to the child, without in the least exploiting him or her, and always maintaining obviously affectionate

♏ SCORPIO ♏

relations with the spouse. Love isn't rationed – there's plenty for three, four, or even more. Of course, it's never easy for Scorpio to face rivalry, and there are sure to be some difficult patches. However, embarrassment and withholding can do damage to any of us, not least young Scorpio. The lesson in managing Scorpio is not to be afraid of feelings, and to be able to be open about those that may be damaging. A Scorpio who sees that his or her parents can cope with things is less likely to repress his or her own 'dark side', and thereby give it power.

Of course, while some little Scorpios can seem precociously sexual, we need to remember that Scorpio is principally interested in intense emotional experience. They are testing out the highs and lows of the human condition and their own capacity for feeling and coping with it all. In the process they may set severe tests for their parents! However, not all little Scorpions are difficult and demanding, by any means. Some are very understanding and will instinctively know when mum or dad need a cuddle. One two-year-old, with a strong Scorpio, spotted his mum crying about a news report of the Dunblane tragedy. 'Dey dere,' he said (i.e. 'stay there'). Off he toddled and came back, moments later, with his own flannel, proceeding to mop up the tears assiduously and tenderly. Can you wonder his mum cried all the more?

Scorpios won't compromise, but they will co-operate, if well handled. Scorpio body – or other – space must be invaded as little as possible and parents need to be alive to the signals that certain attention isn't wanted. Needless to say, Scorpios should never be 'forced' to eat their dinner (want to try it?) and their objections to certain clothes or habits should be listened to as soon as they can express them, and accommodated as much as is feasible. This is about respect, which Scorpio understands, and if they are given it they will render it. If not, they will get their own way in the end, by fair means or the

♏ All in the family ♏

foulest. Scorpio toddlers may show vengeful behaviour – but so can most children. They should be treated firmly and kindly. However, it is possible that Scorpio may have phobias, or a morbid imagination, and all these things will need to be talked through and given the greatest understanding. Little Scorpios are often great sleuths, finding things the family have lost, and they may be true to their sign in a taste for horror films and ghost stories. However, some Scorpios are very frightened by such things and should be protected from all such until they feel ready to deal with them.

Young Scorpio can sometimes be manipulated by guilt or misdirected by family undercurrents. More likely a Scorpio who feels that her or his parents have 'plans' will do a great deal to thwart them, and they may thwart themselves in the process. At the least, they are likely to make a bid for early freedom. One Scorpio girl, hearing her mum say she was 'glad she had a daughter because it would mean there was someone who could look after her in her old age' made a mental note to set up home as far as possible, as soon as possible, and in the event took up residence on the other side of the globe!

The wild winds of adolescence may be hurricanes with Scorpio. There isn't much you can do about this, for Scorpio will learn to cope. Never probe – Scorpios must have their secrets – but do be available with advice, support and understanding. Never judge their behaviour and try to be as open-minded as possible about sexual activity. Occasionally, Scorpio will put off intimate sexual encounter, realising this is a momentous thing, but more usually experimentation will be irresistible and this will be far safer if parents are open and accepting, so their advice about safe methods can be listened to. Scorpio is canny about human nature, and only the minimum of warnings should be necessary – this sign tends to take risks mainly when there is something to prove. As Scorpio grows up, the turbulent adolescent will be replaced by a wise and profound adult, an eternal and loyal friend to all who have helped and supported. With any luck mum and dad will be the best friends of all.

■ SCORPIO AS SIBLING

The most disconcerting thing about a Scorpio brother or sister can be that they know all their siblings' secrets, and some they never knew they had! This is especially tough if Scorpio is the youngest. Often this is best solved by taking Scorpio into their confidence and enlisting help. Scorpio will never betray siblings, unless they are *really* mean. Then it won't matter anyway, because Scorpio will be serialising their private journal in the school magazine, however well they hide it.

Sometimes siblings may need to be careful who they complain about, or young Scorpio may hide a worm in their best friend's socks, just because they let it slip that he or she hadn't returned that book the brother or sister lent them. Scorpios, whether older or younger, can be trusty champions. Like most born under the sign, they are a wonderful friend and a dangerous enemy. Mostly, however, Scorpios are pleasant, and even quite bland. The depths of many Scorpios are not evident, and this may be because they have been treated with affection and consideration – always the best course with all of us!

■ SCORPIO IN THE HOME

Of paramount importance to Scorpio is privacy. Naturally Scorpios will want their own room, but if this is not possible, at least make sure they have a desk, cupboard or even casket that they can lock. Never rummage around in Scorpio's possessions, for they like to feel they are respected. If a room has to be shared make sure that the available space is apportioned so no one feels invaded.

♏ All in the family ♏

Cupboards should not be shared, curtains can be strategically placed and lighting should be subtle and clever, so that each person can read or do other things without disturbing the other. Scorpios will often like to have a 'den' perhaps under their bed and a personal stereo with earphones is a good idea because Scorpios can then enter their own world. Bunks are not recommended. Feng shui experts say these are not advisable, and it is hard to have privacy if someone is above or below you. Scorpio is not usually a sign that needs to sprawl everywhere – the most important thing is that Scorpios feel they have their own domain, upon which no one else will intrude. They do also need to be encouraged to respect the privacy of others, and this is, like most things, best learnt by example.

♏ SCORPIO ♏

■ PRACTICE AND CHANGE ■

- Honesty, especially of the emotional variety, is definitely the best policy in any Scorpio household. Feelings should be faced and openly expressed as much as possible. This doesn't mean by shouting, stamping and throwing. It means discussing. Scorpionic transformations can be achieved only by working with what is going on, not trying to ignore it.
- Be very aware of any 'control' issues and ensure that each person receives autonomy and respect. Scorpio needs this and also may need to be reminded to accord it.
- Scorpios pick up undercurrents. If Scorpio is behaving badly it may be wise to look at the environment.
- Scorpio parents may need to remind themselves that they will not spoil their child or render her or him vulnerable by displays of affection. They do not need to repress their feelings. A child who knows they are loved is a child who has fathomless strength, in the end.
- In addition, Scorpios need to be prepared to reward *themselves* by closeness and cuddles.
- The autonomy and privacy of Scorpio children must be respected from as early an age as possible. Be firm on occasion, but always understanding.
- Parents of Scorpios should learn not to be worried or thrown by the intensity of this child. Be aware of subliminal messages that may say to the child 'Don't get too close', 'Don't want too much love'. We are all at our best if given what we need, and to Scorpio this particularly applies.

4 Friendships and the single life

> *And let there be no purpose in friendship save the
> deepening of the spirit.
> For love that seeks aught but the disclosure of its own
> mystery is not love but a net cast forth:
> and only the unprofitable is caught*
>
> Kahlil Gibran, *The Prophet*

Naturally friendships are important to all of us, but those who do not have partners may find we have more time to spend with friends. Scorpio puts a great deal into partnerships and may become absorbed in them. However, this sign never forgets old friends and will be eager to take up with them once more when the emotional climate has cooled a little.

■ SCORPIO AS A FRIEND

There are rarely half-measures with Scorpio and if you have decided to trust friends and let them close, you are capable of giving a great deal. You can nearly always be relied upon to lend them a sympathetic ear and scour your mind and heart for resourceful and empathic advice. Sometimes you will know how friends are feeling, and what they are going to say. A Scorpio friend once phoned me and said 'What's the matter?' She had picked up on the ether that something was amiss, and she was right!

Friends may find themselves telling Scorpio all sorts of things about their past and their most secret feelings. However, while you will take them into your confidence if you have decided they are 'okay',

SCORPIO

there are intimate corners of your soul into which they are rarely admitted. Scorpio isn't good at asking for help and you will sometimes be quite offhand about your troubles. If there is something you abhor it is pity. Friends should show you empathy, however, and you will be more likely to open out. Nonetheless, with all your affection they will sometimes find themselves wondering what you are thinking.

If pressed, Scorpio will give a frank opinion – this sign tells lies only for important matters and you would rather not insult friends with a euphemism if their behaviour at that party where they got totally out of their head really was beyond the pale. However, this sign is not given to brutal frankness, either. You do not want to hurt them and so you will avoid passing on upsetting information if this isn't useful. However, if you see a friend's lover out with someone else or have heard that the company a friend works for is about to collapse, you will tell them, feeling that they need the knowledge. In their position you would far rather know, because 'forewarned is forearmed'. You will stand by their side while they fight.

Scorpions are always their 'own person' and you like friends to be their own person too. Weeping willows you can cope with, but clinging vines are another matter. Yours is a sign that must have space, so friends should not invade it. Probably they need their's, too, or they wouldn't be your friends in the first place. Much is made of Scorpionic 'strength' and 'domination' but you can be a most passive companion, moulding into the background where appropriate. At a dinner party given by a friend, a Scorpio guest helped to serve the meal and arrange the giggling mass of the other guests in their places. 'When you're entertaining,' commented our hostess to me later, 'the last thing you want is someone who'll think for themselves. The great thing about Sandie is she doesn't ask questions – she just does what you say!' Here the empathy of Scorpio and respect for the decisions of others comes into play.

Friendships and the single life

Much is made of Scorpionic vengefulness, and I am sure that there are no second chances if others really let you down. However, Scorpionic kindness and support is much more characteristic, and you are a loyal person on whom friends can rely. After many years of friendship there will still be little things they can find out about you – it makes you interesting and adds to your mystique and value. Hearts worn on the sleeve become faded and insipid, but Scorpio's always beats strong, deep in the chest.

SCORPIO AND THE SINGLE LIFE

Scorpios often enjoy being alone, for it gives you more time to probe and remake yourselves and to delve into any and every mystery that fascinates you, without having anyone breathing down your neck. It has to be said that some Scorpios do like to live alone because you are secretive and find it too hard to let anyone that close – and occasionally you may have something to hide, or imagine you have. This, however, is rare. While Scorpio does enjoy and need space, in time you can become quite desperate for passionate contact and will even take risks to find this. This is a Water sign, and correspondingly emotional. With Scorpio it is always a balancing act to achieve both intensity in relationships and also plenty of room to be yourself and explore yourself.

Some Scorpios purposely wound themselves by self-imposed loneliness because they have somehow taken the idea of original sin into their core and feel they are rotten and unfit for company. This, of course, is utter rubbish, and it stems merely from the fact that the Scorpion is usually more honest with itself and cannot hide feelings and desires that more superficial people would blithely pretend they do not have.

♏ SCORPIO ♏

Lone Scorpios often find that fateful or dramatic things happen to them, such as meeting a poet on a train and striking up an unforgettable relationship. On the whole, Scorpios who aren't in a partnership do need to have very meaningful associations with intimate friends where they can have soul contact. If you are a Scorpio and you find yourself on your own, ask yourself what you have always wanted to get to grips with, learn about, get to the bottom of. Have you wanted time to develop your psychic potential, your artistic talent, your scope of knowledge? Now is your chance, but before you slam the castle door and pull up the drawbridge, give yourself the chance to establish one or two friendships with people with whom you can discuss at least some of the things that really matter to you.

♏ Friendships and the single life ♏

■ PRACTICE AND CHANGE ■

- If you have decided to call someone 'friend' then be prepared to let this person help you, if you need it.
- If you hurt, manipulate and use you will be the loser. Think positive thoughts, if you are able, of rebuilding and remaking. In time you will come to see that to 'Live well is the best revenge'.
- Remember to maintain steady contact with friends. Not everyone has your changeless approach, and while you may 'know' the friendship is always there, others may not have your instincts and may need reassurance.
- Although you care deeply about your friends they do have to make their own mistakes. You cannot remake them or live their lives for them even though you can see so clearly what course they should take. It may be painful to stand by and watch, but that is all you can do. Your regenerative ability will be invaluable when it comes to picking up the pieces and starting again.
- If you are alone this does not mean that you are 'too bad for company' – it may be that you are too good for it, in some ways, and that you seek a depth of encounter that most cannot match. However, some can, and you will find them in time. You don't need me to remind you 'unto thine own self be true'.
- Time alone is a prime opportunity to get down to doing whatever it is that you have really wanted to do. Take this opportunity. Doing what you need and want to do creates a magnetic atmosphere that in time draws suitable companions to you.

5 ♏ Career

Few men ... come anywhere near exhausting the resources dwelling within them. There are deep wells of strength which are never used

Admiral Richard Byrd

The quiet Scorpionic exterior may convince many people that this person is laid back, doesn't care much for esteem, personal advancement or money, and is generally as contented as a grazing sheep – but do not be deceived! Scorpio burns with ambition, likes power and requires money for a feeling of security. The more money, the greater the security – a simple equation.

However, many Scorpios seek something more subtle from their chosen occupation, and there is often a need to contribute something of meaning to society, or to face things that are shunned by many. You occasionally sacrifice yourselves for a cause, but not in the sense of merging and total identification with the unfortunate or victimised that is more frequently associated with Pisces. With Scorpio it is more a knowledge that someone has to do this, go there, face that, and the pure fact is that you are capable, while others are not. You may feel at home in situations which others might find gruesome, revolting or frightening, and so you sometimes choose gruelling careers, such as work with the doubly incontinent, severely disabled or dying. This is rarely a superficial sign, and many Scorpios are dedicated in some way, some to a cause, some to their art or to scientific advancement, and most of you are thorough with a steak of perfectionism in your approach.

♏ Career ♏

■ TRADITIONAL SCORPIO CAREERS

Scorpio careers include:

- surgeon
- psychoanalyst
- research
- analysis
- detective or police work
- armed forces
- undertaker
- physicist
- butcher
- scientist
- lawyer
- coroner
- occult investigator
- healer
- pathologist
- sewage worker
- pharmacist
- medium
- insurance worker
- key positions in big business

■ WHAT TO LOOK FOR IN YOUR WORK

The common denominator with all occupations suitable for Scorpios is that they involve dealing with the nitty-gritty, the basics of life which are not very cosmetic and are sometimes downright scary, and they involve going 'below the surface' in some way.

The great majority of people work in large insurance corporations, sales offices, shops, banks and factories. Relatively few of us can choose a profession, train for it and find a fulfilling lifestyle, and as time progresses this is becoming more elusive.

To help you find a job that suits you, you need to bear in mind the spirit of what is recommended, not the specific occupation. One office job is not like another, one shop selling fashions may differ enormously from one down the street in terms of environment and opportunity. As a Scorpio you need to make sure of several things when seeking employment:

- There is a reasonable amount of security to be had from your position, in terms of money and also in regard to location and such like. You will not relish frequent moves, unless you are in control of them.
- Your job requires commitment. A take-it-or-leave-it type of job is not likely to be for you – you need to feel that some demands are made upon you and that you are needed by people.
- You have some autonomy and decision-making power of your own, or at least the prospect of this.
- What you do has a sense of meaning – that is, it must mean something at a level deeper than the trivial or a job done just for the sake of the salary.
- Good money is important to you, and while you may be prepared to work your way patiently to a position of wealth, you are aware that money is power.
- What you do should engage you at a deep level. It should call on your wellsprings and resources, and should challenge you to give of your best at a fundamental level.

So there is no need to feel that you have to look for a specifically Scorpionic job. Many Scorpios would be revolted by work as a butcher or soldier and profoundly sceptical of mediumship. Look for something that suits in its content and atmosphere, rather than its label. Check things out before you commit yourself.

THE SPHYNX

Strange as it may seem, the Sphynx rarely has the inscrutable air of one who has spent an eternity gazing upon the 'lone and level sands' and who possesses incommunicable knowledge about human life and all that lies beyond it. No, the Sphynx often has a bland and quite ordinary exterior, friendly and ready to chat. The

♏ Career ♏

Sphynx may be sympathetic and helpful concerning all the trials and tribulations to which employed flesh is heir, and nothing nefarious or even mildly mysterious lurks behind their twinkling gaze. After a while, however, colleagues may realise that while they have told this person all their family history, the Sphynx has never told them one thing about his or her own background, or ever criticised the job in any way, shape or form.

This is the most dangerous kind of Scorpio, but before colleagues don armour plating and head for the hills in a panic, they should just read on a little. The Sphynx means no harm and it is most unlikely that anything said to this person will go any further – he or she will be as trustworthy with comments as with any other piece of information. In addition, the kind demeanour of the Sphynx was probably totally genuine, and would have been backed up with some real help, and had it been needed. However, two things should be remembered. The Sphynx is probably heading steadily for the door going somewhere else that fits his or her private agenda, and will get there, come hell or high water. Second, if colleagues ever try to hurt, thwart or demean this person, they have given him or her an arsenal – and it will be used, make no mistake. Make a friend of the Sphynx, for he or she could be a good one, but never an enemy – and learn from her or him the advisability of discretion!

■ THE BLACK WIDOW

This sounds the nastiest type anyone could meet, and indeed, at first glance the Black Widow spins a creepy, extensive web and is dangerously poisonous. Black Widow hears all the whispers down the corridors of power, crawling into positions of confidence and influence, ready to tweak that straggling web and go in for the kill when the time is right. Black Widow has been known to exploit the vulnerable and even to take what does not belong to him or her. In addition, this person has a ready sting, able to cut colleagues to the quick with a razor-sharp word, should they step out of line – or should he or she feel like it.

Sounds sinister? Well, maybe, but Black Widow often has a charming exterior, all the better for being so easily seen through. This type is the most blatant and by far the least powerful of Scorpios because it is so obvious what they are about. Colleagues can throw them some juicy titbits if they want to amuse themselves, and get on with life. And if you are the teeniest-weeniest Black Widowy yourself, what on earth are you doing wasting all your subtlety, penetration and power on being nasty and manipulative? You can certainly do better than that. Shred that web and build another that really means something, before you get truly fed up with life.

THE SCORPIO BOSS

This boss probably likes his or her employees, or they wouldn't be working for him or her – Scorpios don't readily tolerate the proximity of anyone their instincts have not given the thumbs up. Employees can rely on sympathy, understanding and support, but Pluto help them if they lie – this boss will know. They would do better to own up and ask for a few moments to discuss their problems – Scorpio boss may well have some sound advice, and be deeply empathic.

Employees may be an open book to their Scorpio boss, but he or she is as inscrutable as a medieval grimoire. They should not probe or question the motives of this person, for they will get nowhere, except perhaps nearer the door. Most of all, they should never insult their boss's pride or criticise – helpful comments are one thing, criticism is another, and Scorpio will never forget. If employees want to get inside the 'magic circle' they should not oppose this boss. Neither should they be misled by the cool exterior into thinking this is Ms or Mr Laid Back, because when crisis strikes the black lake will turn into a raging torrent, generating enough hydro-electric power to light a city – and often switching off again just as suddenly. Scorpio can be full of surprises.

If employees choose to compliment their Scorpio boss they should make sure it is sincere – flannel will make him or her deeply suspicious. Most important of all, they should never deceive. They probably won't get away with it unless they're very good – even the most penetrating Scorpio doesn't see everything. Most importantly, this boss responds best to loyalty, honesty and support. Despite the ruthless streak, the most notable thing about Scorpio is humanity. If employees find themselves in a tight corner, their Scorpio boss will fight for them with all that considerable intensity if they have shown that they are firmly behind him or her. Scorpio respects feelings – if employees always respect their boss's, with any luck they will have as an ally someone who wields steadily increasing power.

THE SCORPIO EMPLOYEE

This is a thorough, reliable and honest worker who is often as committed to work as he or she is non-committal about everything else – ambitions, private life, preferences – Scorpio looks as if he or she can take it or leave it while being the original willing horse. By now, of course, you will be aware that this is only skin-deep, but this is one smooth, impenetrable membrane. Scorpio can put resentments on ice or even forget them altogether if they may stand in the way of that goal, whatever it may be. This person can even swallow pride and if that gets the desired objective, it will rarely even cause indigestion. However, before employers think they can get away with anything with this person, demand that Scorpio works twelve hours a day, all weekend and takes a drop in salary, they had best be quite sure they know what Scorpio wants – and that is no easy matter. Scorpio only suffers for a reason, and while that may seem obscure, to Scorpio it is clearly defined. If employers'

♏ SCORPIO ♏

demands do not serve this reason then that, as they say, is that – with a vengeance.

This employee is a person to value, for Scorpios are usually creative, resourceful, loyal and capable of giving 101 per cent. Probably what Scorpio wants in the end is some form of power. This may mean money, position or something more subtle, such as autonomy or creative freedom. Deep inside Scorpio there is usually a bell-like voice that repeats 'Unto thine own self be true' and Scorpio listens. Scorpios never forget those who have been a help. However, they *may* just forget unfair demands if this has been a price they have *chosen* to pay. Of course, employers can never be sure, so best treat this person fairly. If Scorpios have decided they want something they usually get it, and it could be uncomfortable if a mistreated underling becomes MD in a few years. On the other hand, prize this private, intense and talented individual for what he or she is and employers will have an ally for life.

■ WHEN UNEMPLOYMENT STRIKES

This fixed sign can be badly shaken by unemployment and you certainly worry a great deal about interrupted income, which is a severe threat to security. Many Scorpios are 'control freaks' in some sense and thus feel deeply unsettled when forces beyond their control zap their life out of orbit.

Having said this, however, you will rarely admit you are frightened and vulnerable, and others may have to guess at the trauma by the fact that you have gone quiet, or have taken to repeating 'It will be all right, there are ways of coping,' in a lilting tone that could deceive a telepath. At this time you need help, but you may have trouble accepting it. Offers of loans tend to be politely declined and platitudes fall on deaf ears. However, Scorpio appreciates offers of support, even if they are not taken up.

It is a help to you to be reminded how well you have coped in the past and to recall that there are many talents that you have not exploited. You need to be helped to help yourself, or you run the risk of losing self-respect as well as job. The advantages for Scorpio in this sort of situation are several. For instance, although you detest change imposed from without, no one is more capable of self-regeneration than this sign. This may be a prime opportunity for a complete change of direction and lifestyle. Ask yourself what you have wanted to do but perhaps always assumed wasn't possible/ too much of an upheaval or risk. Might this now be possible? Why not consider a fundamental change such as emigration or a job utterly different from all you have tried before?

In an uncertain situation the tough get going, and Scorpio is the toughest of all. Resourceful, courageous and determined, there is no doubt that Scorpio can turn this distressing situation into one that will be beneficial.

■ SELF-EMPLOYMENT AND OTHER MATTERS

Not all work relies on a company and an employer, for there are many other approaches. Scorpio is self-reliant and self-motivating and in many ways is ideally suited to self-employed or freelance work. This sign possesses imagination and perception, but there is also a grain of practicality. This is not the utilitarian approach of the Earth signs but a very basic realisation of life's necessities and how to manage them – Scorpio is often a good 'manager' in some sphere. The only possible pitfalls for the self-employed Scorpio may be loneliness – Scorpio usually needs human contact – and possibly depression when things get problematic. Ensure there are lively and understanding companions to lighten the load.

■ PRACTICE AND CHANGE ■

- When choosing a job, remember that it is important to you to contribute something of value that draws on your deepest resources – financial reward by itself will not do.
- Trying to control everything in life is a recipe for paranoia and neurosis. Learn to 'let go' and have an abiding faith in your own resources and ability to cope.
- Power comes from inner strength and self-knowledge. Your ways are naturally subtle and secret, but do not let this extend to the devious and manipulative. Do not mistrust others – trust yourself.
- Trust is an important factor in your life, especially in your work. Always be prepared to give it, and associate with those who are worth it and who will give it in return.
- Don't take things too seriously – things really don't matter that much, in the long run. Ask yourself how much this is going to matter ten years from now and take it from there.
- Try not to work too intensely – all work and no play won't make the best of your abilities.
- Let yourself take a little help when offered. This will not put you in anyone's power.
- Hang on to your faith in yourself if you find yourself without a job, temporarily. Be prepared to change and approach this creatively.
- If you choose self-employment, do not disappear inside yourself. You need outside interests and other stimulation, or you may become obsessive or blinkered. Give yourself the optimum environment for creativity.

6 Healthy, wealthy – and wise?

There is a remedy for all things but death

Sixteenth-century proverb

■ HEALTH

Astrological observations on health, even when based on the entire birthchart, may be of doubtful value or accuracy, because health depends on so many complex factors. What may we usefully say about the health of Scorpio in general?

One of the principal roads to illness for Scorpio is that of the stoic. Scorpios may tell themselves that trivial symptoms should not bother them, and many will soldier on, even when feeling very low and suffering from several complaints. You often have a high pain threshold and considerable willpower, and you will repress problems when you choose. In addition, you don't like to seek help and yours is one of the signs rather prone to say they 'don't want to bother the doctor'. Because of this you risk periodic complete breakdowns in health, when you are laid low for several days or weeks. However, your recuperative powers are phenomenal, and Scorpio is the sign perhaps most capable of hauling itself back from the very brink even of death and of continuing with recharged vigour and enthusiasm. The phoenix again!

Although you rarely deceive yourself in any major way about how you feel (in fact you may 'face up' to weaknesses you do not really have) we have seen that you frequently choose to keep the bulk of your feelings to yourself. Sexual frustration is especially hard on Scorpio as you need intense contact with a loved human being. However, many Scorpios do endure this, and even opt for celibacy, for several reasons, including maintenance of total control over their lives. Without the release of sexual passion, stress can build in this sign to a point where it is detrimental to health. In addition, Scorpio often finds it hard to discharge emotions, 'maggotting away' with resentments and suspicions, to the point where you are almost poisoning your system. Some Scorpios are obsessive. All Scorpios need to learn to express their feelings in some fashion rather than risk this subtle self-destruction.

Scorpio, as an emotional Water sign, is usually acutely aware of the feelings of others. Scorpios do well to choose companions with care, associating with people who are capable of empathy and honesty, and who will create a climate where Scorpio can feel at least reasonably safe in expressing needs and feelings. Scorpio, despite the strength of the sign, is affected by the moods of others to a great degree, and if someone near is perpetually moody, demanding, resentful and angry, Scorpio often feels strangely guilty and responsible. In such cases you need to put the responsibility back squarely where it belongs. If not, such circumstances can also be hard on health, creating possible anxiety and depression.

There is no sign more capable of recuperating and regenerating than the Scorpion and it seems almost that you 'make yourself' ill at times in order to go through a process of 'rebirth'.

The lower bowel, bladder and genitals

Scorpio is said to 'rule' the sexual and excretory organs, and this certainly seems appropriate for a sign closely linked to all forms of elimination and regrowth. It is possible that Scorpio may be prone to constipation, and I have also heard of cases where the bladder did not empty properly. Psychologically this may be linked to a wish to control and 'hold back'. Louise Hay, in *You Can Heal Your Life*, links bladder problems to anxiety, a fear of letting go, irritability and dissatisfaction. There is no doubt that the bowel reacts powerfully to the way we feel, and it is certainly possible that anyone who is 'emotionally constipated' may become physically bound up, too, for the bladder is also linked to control. Scorpios who experience this need to learn to relax and seek out situations and people that make them feel safe. Any condition of this sort may make us more prone to infection, so in addition to proper attention to diet Scorpio also needs to learn to relax, and massage and aromatherapy are naturally beneficial for this.

Scorpio, being cautious and circumspect, is not more prone to venereal disease than other signs. However, it is interesting to note that the emergence of AIDS has coincided with the passage of the 'Underworld' planet, Pluto, through its own sign of Scorpio. This has brought to our attention many Scorpionic themes, such as how we manage our sexuality. In some quarters this has given rise to mutterings about a biblical retribution, and very sadly a condemnation of the gay community. More appropriately, we might link the spread of AIDS to the lack of respect for the sacred nature of the sexual act, for sex is an act of worship and a gift of the Mother Goddess. This perspective is equally ignored both by repressive morality and by exploitative pornography, which some people see as two sides of the same coin. These are Scorpionic motifs indeed.

■ MONEY

Generally this is a thrifty sign, needing, for security, to have finances under control and well planned. Money is a form of power, and Scorpio likes to wield, not be at the mercy of, power.

♏ SCORPIO ♏

You find it hard to put money worries to the back of your mind, and often your self-control is exemplary. However, just occasionally, you may see something you just 'have to have' and then all good resolutions and healthy bank balances may be whistled down the wind! Usually, Scorpio recuperates well in this sphere as in all others, but it can be quite stressful on the system.

Scorpio is linked in traditional astrology to insurance, especially life assurance. Scorpios with families may be quite heavily insured – this is not usually an improvident sign. Tradition also suggests that Scorpio may be fortunate with inheritance.

Occasionally, this sign can be rather mean with money, and I have even heard of one Scorpio parent who charged his children interest on money he loaned them, which is one tough way to learn about life! However, a secure Scorpio is capable of generosity with friends and family. Most Scorpios are quite upfront about finances, arranging without embarrassment who is going to pay for what.

■ WISDOM

Scorpios are often deeply wise individuals who are able to see human nature for what it is – yours is one of the hardest signs to fool, one of the most sceptical and aware. You know that there are inner and more profound meanings to everything. Prepared to face circumstances that others may shun, you can be found helping the dying, the ill or psychologically disturbed with a fearlessness that stems from having a vivid sense of the totality of existence. You reclaim the shadowlands, seeing them not as places of revulsion but as repositories of the divine. One might say that Scorpio sees with the gut, accepting the reality of the human condition with its suffering and tribulation and also the potential for the sublime that exists within all. Because of this Scorpio can be a most heartening and encouraging influence and a source of deep wisdom.

■ PRACTICE AND CHANGE ■

Health

- You may need to 'play hard' to release tension – make provision for this.
- Try to release your feelings when they are eating away at you.
- Choose your associates with care. Be aware of how you may be taking the feelings of others on board. Try to keep the company of empathic and aware people, where possible. If you have to be with those who affect you in this way, try a simple cleansing ritual such as a bath with lavender water, where you visualise all the contamination washing away, or light a joss stick and affirm that the scented smoke is expunging all unwanted emotions.
- Remember you *do not have to lay low to regenerate*. Choose to regenerate yourself by an act of will, or rituals such as simple candle burning and affirming the bright flame is transmuting what needs to change, as the flame changes the wax. Strenuous exercise, where compatible with health is also an excellent 'regenerator'.

Wealth

- Try to loosen up a little about money. In reasonable circumstances it will always be possible for you to create the wealth you need.
- You cannot possibly be prepared for everything. Do your best, forget the rest.
- Don't beat yourself up internally if you have overspent. You deserved a treat. If you do not get pleasure out of it, now that is a waste. Enjoy!

7 Style and leisure

Moderation is a fatal thing... Nothing succeeds like excess. The only way to get rid of a temptation is to yield to it.

Oscar Wilde

■ YOUR LEISURE

As a Scorpio you have a great need to unwind, because you generally put all of yourself and more into what you do. Working hard should be followed by playing hard, and for this you will need to do something that engages you passionately and deeply, and arouses all of your interest. Many Scorpios are drawn to anything mysterious and 'mystery' games and sleuthing may appeal. Some also like psychic investigating and 'ghost hunting' – at least those occupations are some of the traditional attributions of the sign. Few self-respecting ghosts will be caught in that way, as most sensible Scorpios will be aware. Nonetheless, it is always fascinating to Scorpio to be on the trail of the arcane, the magical and the obscure. Some also like horror films, sci-fi and detective films or stories – although again there are Scorpios who abhor the 'horrific' as they are too acutely aware of the presence of such phenomena beneath the veneer of everyday life. Occasionally, you are drawn to charity work, but care needs to be taken here that you are not motivated by some feeling of guilt or need to expiate that is not built on reality. You need to engage in something that is deeply enjoyable to you, for its own sake.

Scorpio can certainly go to extremes and this may be anything from eating binges to sexual indulgence. With sensible limits this can be

♏ Style and leisure ♏

a good thing, for such experience can be cathartic, for you must not deny yourself a vivid interaction with life. The point here is not that it is okay to do what you like regardless of drawbacks or the feelings of others but to have an absorbing, saturating and renewing episode. The dangers, apart from the obvious, can be that such 'extremes' are followed by periods of denial, and then followed in turn by excess. It is better to have a little of what you fancy – or better still a lot of what you fancy – on a regular basis.

The old ruler of Scorpio was Mars, and the Martian energy is evident in some members of the sign. These may enjoy demanding sports that require physical endurance and concentration such as ultra-distance running or marathons. You can be very competitive and good at one-to-one sports – possibly wrestling, boxing or martial arts. You are not usually so good at team sports unless you are a leader, for you may find it hard to fit in with the requirements of others. Exercise is good for all of us and can be a beneficial release – swimming is especially recommended.

If you are a Scorpio looking for a fresh interest or a hobby think first of all whether you wish for something sedentary or active, or what, indeed, would be most beneficial for your health. If you wish to be active then you have the stamina and determination to rebuild yourself, physically, if you so wish. If you have been inactive you should seek qualified advice before embarking on a new regime. You may like exercising alone, to music, you may wish to try weight training or deep-sea diving, swimming with the dolphins or hang gliding – here the Martian enterprise and the 'eagle' side of Scorpio can find expression. If you wish for something sedentary you might enjoy researching your family tree, local history, unsolved crimes or mysteries, archaeology and anything that involves 'digging away' at the hidden. Many Scorpios are passionate about art, literature and music and may be very creative in a highly individualistic way. Also, as we have observed several times, Scorpio does like to get to the bottom of her or himself and may like to embark on psychoanalysis. The only problem here can be that this involves the revelation of oneself to an outsider. Some Scorpios are interested in astrology, graphology and psychological testing.

Holidays

This Fixed sign can be lazy and luxurious and may thoroughly relish soaking up the sun, especially near the sea or large lakes, reading Whodunnits or tales of passion and adventure. Scorpio always likes privacy, or at least the opportunity for being alone when necessary. In addition, despite the native stoicism, this rarely extends to holidays when Scorpio will like to be comfortable. Thus, camping is rarely a good idea, unless it is somewhere exceptionally beautiful and offering a mystical participation in the natural.

Scorpio will not enjoy doing nothing for long, and there should be an ingredient of the exotic or intriguing. Many Scorpios like to tour historical sites and may have a fascination for prehistoric monuments, castles and museums, seeing here not dry relics but a throbbing and mysterious link to other times and other lives. As with anything else connected to this sign, holidays should be a memorable experience. Some Scorpios will enjoy active holidays involving lots of walking or perhaps incorporating a course on art or history. Look for the stimulating, the unusual, the absorbing.

YOUR STYLE

Scorpionic style is about the most difficult of all to encapsulate, for no one is more able than Scorpio to put up a smoke screen. Thus, while it may be natural, in many ways, for Scorpio to be drawn to the

♏ Style and leisure ♏

vivid, bold, exotic and fascinating, many Scorpios go for neutrals and amorphous design in order to preserve their privacy. While some may have the confidence to power-dress or choose individual and dramatic clothes, others wear greys, browns and canvas colours, or simple classics. Whatever design Scorpio chooses it is usually for a purpose and the Scorpio makes an impression upon observers.

Scorpios usually like their clothes to be serviceable and 'definite' with an emphasis on strong, quality fabrics and elegant tailoring. Extravert Scorpios like their clothes to be a personality statement. Where seduction is the game, no one knows how to play it better than Scorpio, with leathers, black lace and musky fragrance. On other occasions Scorpios will prefer to be practical and dressed for whatever action they are engaged upon. Female Scorpios can make like a vamp, with long, red nails and lipstick, or like a mouse, in a faded tracksuit. The males may wear the executive suit of the city slicker or old jeans. Unless it suits their purpose they are rarely bothered by what other people think. Some Scorpios choose a bohemian style that is colourful and glamorous, and as such come into their dramatic best. Blacks, dark reds and greens or neutral colours may be the favourites.

Scorpio living space usually has a traditional flavour with solid wood furniture, unusual artefacts and natural substances such as earthenware, basketwork and leather. There may be many books and some objects that are hard to identify so you have to look and ask. Rich colours and designs in dark colours are often chosen and Scorpios do not always choose to have a lot of light in their surroundings. There may be a preference for a house with beams or lots of plants with foliage that filters the glare. Scorpio will not want to be exposed and so net curtains may be used, although they are a little fussy for the sign. Anything not chosen for interest or beauty will need to be serviceable and durable. Scorpios often enjoy having a

SCORPIO

good sort out, for this can be cathartic, and there will need to be a bin for items to be recycled and a bag for the charity shop.

When you are choosing purchases for yourself or your home think strong, serviceable, subtle/dramatic, evocative, atmospheric, mysterious, fascinating, durable, useful, traditional, interesting. Do not let the fact that you value what is lasting and useful keep you from the dramatic and exotic, for you will probably relish that, too.

■ PRACTICE AND CHANGE ■

- Look for absorbing pastimes – the superficial may not hold your interest or relax you. Make time to 'throw yourself' into a pastime.
- Don't try too hard to be 'moderate'. You need a little excess here and there in order to feel really alive.
- Make a note that you will give yourself the time to explore more fully at least one subject that you have always wondered about.
- Your holidays need to be relaxing and absorbing. Consider comfort, privacy and/or something that makes demands on you like a course in screen printing, bird watching, simply walking or observing wildlife.
- If you are a Scorpio who has always chosen neutrals, try something more flamboyant to give you a lift.
- Turning out your cupboards is great therapy – why not give it a try, some rainy day?
- Your living area needs to offer you what you need in life – privacy. Consider seriously any changes you might make to increase this, if it is not satisfactory at present.

Appendix 1

▪ SCORPIO COMBINED WITH MOON SIGN

Our 'birth sign' or 'star sign' refers to the sign of the zodiac occupied by the Sun when we were born. This is also called our 'Sun sign' and this book is concerned with Scorpio as a Sun sign. However, as we saw in the Introduction, a horoscope means much more than the position of the Sun alone. All the other planets have to be taken into consideration by an astrologer. Of great importance is the position of the Moon.

The Moon completes a tour of the zodiac in about twenty-eight days, changing sign every two days or so. The Moon relates to our instincts, responses, reactions, habits, comfort zone and 'where we live' emotionally – and sometimes physically. It is very important in respect of our intuitional abilities and our capacity to feel part of our environment, but because what the Moon rules is usually non-verbal and non-rational, it has been neglected. This has meant that our lives have become lop-sided. Learning to be friends with our instincts can lead to greater well-being and wholeness.

Consult the table on page 80 to find which sign the Moon was in, at the time of your birth. This, combined with your Sun sign is a valuable clue to deeper understanding.

♏ SCORPIO ♏

Find your Moon number

Look up your month and day of birth. Then read across to find your personal Moon number. Now go to Chart 2, below.

January		February		March		April		May		June	
1,2	1	1,2	3	1,2	3	1,2	5	1,2	6	1,2	8
3,4	2	3,4	4	3,4	4	3,4	6	3,4	7	3,4	9
5,6	3	5,6	5	5,6	5	5,6	7	5,6	8	5,6,7	10
7,8	4	7,8	6	7,8	6	7,8	8	7,8	9	8,9	11
9,10	5	9,10,11	7	9,10	7	9,10,11	9	9,10	10	10,11,12	12
11,12	6	12,13	8	11,12	8	12,13	10	11,12,13	11	13,14	1
13,14	7	14,15	9	13,14	9	14,15,16	11	14,15,16	12	15,16,17	2
15,16,17	8	16,17,18	10	15,16,17	10	17,18	12	17,18	1	18,19	3
18,19	9	19,20	11	18,19	11	19,20,21	1	19,20	2	20,21	4
20,21	10	21,22,23	12	20,21,22	12	22,23	2	21,22,23	3	22,23	5
22,23,24	11	24,25	1	23,24,25	1	24,25	3	24,25	4	24,25	6
25,26	12	26,27,28	2	26,27	2	26,27,28	4	26,27	5	26,27	7
27,28,29	1	29	3	28,29	3	29,30	5	28,29	6	28,29,30	8
30,31	2			30,31	4			30,31	7		

July		August		September		October		November		December	
1,2	9	1	10	1,2	12	1,2	1	1,2,3	3	1,2	4
3,4	10	2,3	11	3,4	1	3,4	2	4,5	4	3,4	5
5,6,7	11	4,5,6	12	5,6,7	2	5,6	3	6,7	5	5,6	6
8,9	12	7,8	1	8,9	3	7,8,9	4	8,9	6	7,8,9	7
10,11,12	1	9,10	2	10,11	4	10,11	5	10,11	7	10,11	8
13,14	2	11,12,13	3	12,13	5	12,13	6	12,13	8	12,13	9
15,16	3	14,15	4	14,15	6	14,15	7	14,15	9	14,15	10
17,18	4	16,17	5	16,17	7	16,17	8	16,17,18	10	16,17	11
19,20	5	18,19	6	18,19	8	18,19	9	19,20	11	18,19,20	12
21,22,23	6	20,21	7	20,21,22	9	20,21	10	21,22,23	12	21,22	1
24,25	7	22,23	8	23,24	10	22,23,24	11	24,25	1	23,24,25	2
26,27	8	24,25	9	25,26,27	11	25,26	12	26,27,28	2	26,27	3
28,29	9	26,27,28	10	28,29	12	27,28,29	1	29,30	3	28,29	4
30,31	10	29,30	11	30	1	30,31	2			30,31	5
		31	12								

Find your Moon sign

Find your year of birth. Then read across to the column of your Moon number. Where they intersect shows your Moon sign.

Birth year					1	2	3	4	5	6	7	8	9	10	11	12
1900	1919	1938	1957	1976	Sco	Cap	Pis	Tau	Ari	Gem	Lib	Leo	Vir	Aqu	Sag	Can
1901	1920	1939	1958	1977	Ari	Gem	Lib	Leo	Vir	Aqu	Sag	Can	Cap	Pis	Tau	Sco
1902	1921	1940	1959	1978	Aqu	Sag	Can	Cap	Pis	Sco	Tau	Gem	Lib	Leo	Vir	Ari
1903	1922	1941	1960	1979	Leo	Vir	Ari	Sco	Gem	Lib	Tau	Sag	Aqu	Cap	Pis	Can
1904	1923	1942	1961	1980	Gem	Lib	Tau	Sag	Aqu	Cap	Pis	Sco	Ari	Leo	Vir	Can
1905	1924	1943	1962	1981	Pis	Tau	Sco	Cap	Leo	Ari	Gem	Lib	Sag	Vir	Can	Aqu
1906	1925	1944	1963	1982	Vir	Ari	Gem	Lib	Sag	Vir	Can	Aqu	Sco	Tau	Pis	Cap
1907	1926	1945	1964	1983	Cap	Pis	Leo	Vir	Can	Aqu	Sco	Ari	Tau	Gem	Lib	Sag
1908	1927	1946	1965	1984	Sag	Can	Cap	Pis	Sco	Tau	Gem	Lib	Leo	Vir	Aqu	Ari
1909	1928	1947	1966	1985	Ari	Gem	Lib	Leo	Vir	Aqu	Sag	Can	Cap	Pis	Tau	Sco
1910	1929	1948	1967	1986	Tau	Sco	Ari	Gem	Lib	Leo	Vir	Aqu	Sag	Can	Cap	Pis
1911	1930	1949	1968	1987	Gem	Lib	Leo	Vir	Aqu	Sag	Can	Cap	Pis	Sco	Tau	Ari
1912	1931	1950	1969	1988	Gem	Lib	Tau	Sag	Aqu	Cap	Pis	Sco	Ari	Leo	Vir	Can
1913	1932	1951	1970	1989	Aqu	Sag	Can	Cap	Pis	Sco	Tau	Gem	Lib	Leo	Vir	Ari
1914	1933	1952	1971	1990	Ari	Gem	Lib	Leo	Vir	Aqu	Sag	Can	Cap	Pis	Tau	Sco
1915	1934	1953	1972	1991	Pis	Tau	Sco	Cap	Leo	Ari	Gem	Lib	Sag	Vir	Can	Aqu
1916	1935	1954	1973	1992	Lib	Cap	Sag	Vir	Ari	Pis	Gem	Tau	Can	Aqu	Leo	Sco
1917	1936	1955	1974	1993	Sco	Tau	Gem	Lib	Leo	Vir	Aqu	Sag	Can	Cap	Pis	Ari
1918	1937	1956	1975	1994	Sag	Can	Cap	Pis	Sco	Tau	Gem	Lib	Leo	Vir	Aqu	Ari

Ari Tau Gem Can Leo Vir Lib Sco Sag Cap Aqu Pis

Scorpio Sun / Scorpio Moon

You are a person of extreme intensity and depth. It is very important to you to get what you want, and you show great initiative in this respect. Although you may appear cheery and enthusiastic, this may be because it suits your purpose at times. At your worst you can be secretive, devious and manipulative; at your best you can move mountains. You may not express your feelings but they are extremely strong and you may fear vulnerability, using attack as the best means of defence. Probably you are a very sexual person, and you may use sexual satisfaction as a substitute for other needs, because you have more chance of being in control. You like to be one jump ahead and, because you are intuitive and deep seeing, often you are – some people may find your powers of penetration uncanny, and you do like to get to the bottom of everything. Yes, you can be vindictive and jealous but you can also be courageous, loyal and blisteringly honest with yourself. Believe in your inner power and channel your passions constructively. Dare to show your needs – then you have a chance of getting them met.

Scorpio Sun / Sagittarius Moon

You are a great one for starting projects and sometimes you say more than you intend, so exposing yourself uncomfortably. Part of you wants to hold back and part of you wants to surge forwards, and while you may respond with enthusiasm and optimism it can be hard to follow this through when your cautious side takes over. You may escape from your passions and intense desires into philosophy, joking or escapism of one kind or another. You may try to reason away the parts of you that you do not like, although you will always be aware of the emotional dimension, and you may adopt a religion or belief system to give sense and meaning to your life. You are a deep and potentially spiritual person. You owe it to yourself to find a spiritual path that develops your awareness, not one that controls you with guilt. Meanwhile, enjoy the cheerful, adventurous side – you won't get any trouble you can't handle.

Scorpio Sun/Capricorn Moon

You can be a bit of a 'control freak' and mostly this works well for you. You keep yourself well in check, and you keep your feelings to yourself. Generally, you accomplish much, being ambitious and steadfast, and like the Scouts and Guides your motto is 'be prepared'. You may be addicted to achievement, and it might be all too easy to escape from your passions and needs into a determination to succeed, acquire and control, forgetting to ask yourself what all this is about, and whether the standards you have set yourself are truly your own, and are capable of meeting your deepest needs. The external security which you are busy building will not necessarily make you emotionally secure – this can come only by true self-acceptance, in the privacy of your soul, and then by structuring a life – friends, companions, partners – who can meet your emotional requirements. Sooner or later you will have to dare to be vulnerable – go on, it won't kill you – honestly!

Scorpio Sun/Aquarius Moon

Yours is not the easiest combination, because the impulse you have to know yourself (and thus achieve control and concealment) is at variance with your need to escape your feelings and interact with a wide variety of people. The tension may manifest as outbursts of anger or other strong emotion that makes you angry with yourself, but still does not show how you truly feel or get you any closer to finding inner nourishment. Your unpredictability and intermittent detachment may alienate you from the intensity and intimacy you truly need. You can be passionate about humanitarian and related issues, and your intuition is usually good. Often you are far better at helping others than yourself, but you have determination and application. Use your considerable mental resourcefulness to work out what you need, not what makes others tick. Talk yourself into being comfortable with your own passions and be your own best friend, not everyone else's.

Scorpio Sun / Pisces Moon

Your depth, compassion and intuition are unparalleled. Sometimes you feel open to the world's pain, and it is likely that you will try to do something about this – however, you prefer to help those who are also prepared to help themselves. You are never content with the superficial, and you have both courage and imagination when it comes to understanding human dilemmas and motives. Generally, you are at peace with yourself, although you may feel guilty at times and lose yourself in identifying with what other people want, or in what you 'should' do, in respect of work or other routines, rather than applying your courage and penetration in facing up to what you need to do about *you*. Be openly selfish, rather than manipulating other people by taking on the 'martyr' mantle – which you may do at times. Put yourself first, because in that way you will have far more to give anyone else, and you will feel better.

Scorpio Sun / Aries Moon

Here we have a double Mars emphasis, that can make you a fighter on many levels. You have enterprise and initiative as well as realism. 'Fools rush in where angels fear to tread', but while you may indeed launch yourself at situations you generally know exactly what you are letting yourself in for – you are neither fool nor angel but a person of great courage, although you may often wish you weren't quite so impulsive! You may fend off intense feelings by using anger or sex, and pursuing superficial needs may distract you from the deeper ones. Remember that you do not have to be tough. You need to develop the supreme courage to allow yourself to be dependent at times.

Scorpio Sun/Taurus Moon

Your instincts are strong and often wordless. Possibly you experience strong resonance with the land, the seasons and the 'here and now' – you aren't one for abstractions, preferring the evidence of your senses, the strength of your emotions and the security of knowing you can control both what goes on inside you and outside. It is very important to you to know you can be in control of who and what you need. Your sexuality is likely to be powerful, and you can be possessive and stubborn. You are not always happy with the intensity of your emotions, and would like to control that, too, and you may withdraw as a defence. You like to keep your life path under review. It is important for you to distinguish your true needs from your compulsive urges, and to accept that the only certainty in life is change. Try to go with the flow. Given that the environment is reasonably sound (i.e. you are not in a famine or war zone) the universe will always return to you what is rightfully yours and what you need to survive. Take note of your dreams for they can help.

Scorpio Sun/Gemini Moon

You may get on your own nerves at the way your butterfly mind seems to go off at a tangent just when you were determined to get down to something. Often you resort to talk, talk, talk, instead of true feeling. You may feel frustrated that you do not communicate deeply – you need to speak about what really matters, not around the subject. Generally, you are interested in the affairs of others, either in a superficial way or possibly by showing a profound and detailed interest in the human psyche – but that needs to start with *you*. Your versatility, vivacity and cleverness, combined with your intensity and determination can be a powerful combination indeed, but you can achieve the intimacy and meaningful relationships you wish for only if you first get to the bottom of yourself. Harness your mind to what matters – chances are you have so far only touched the surface of your capabilities.

Scorpio Sun/Cancer Moon

You possess a reasonable degree of inner harmony, and within reason you know how to go about providing yourself with a secure and nourishing environment. You are protective of yourself and others, possessive and usually a very private individual, although your instincts let you know when it is safe and appropriate to let someone close. You do not always feel the need to give rational explanations, but it will help if you can cultivate some detachment and objectivity, for it will improve your communications. Not everyone is as empathic as you. You may be a little overattached to your loved ones, familiar surroundings and creature comforts. Mostly you are helpful to others and sensible with your own resources. Remind yourself to support the adult part of the personality in other people and affirm their individuality, as well as your own, rather than concentrating on the inner 'child'. Always be careful that the needs you are satisfying are in your best interests, not just gratification of superficial desires that can be substitutes for what you truly want. You are a caring, supporting individual – make this count in positive ways.

♏ SCORPIO ♏

Scorpio Sun / Leo Moon

You have a great need for attention, and sometimes this can encourage you to be dramatic and demanding in your behaviour. You have a warm heart, but it needs plenty of 'feeding' and if this is not forthcoming you can be domineering and attention seeking. You are a proud individual and find it hard to yield. Thus, you can be stubborn and self-destructive, but you can also show an indomitable will. Your internal need to play and be spontaneous may be at cross-purposes with your wish to seek vivid and meaningful experience. Also your need for privacy may militate against the need to be centre stage. Because of the resulting tension you may overdo things, make demands and create scenes, none of which get you what you really need. You are a strong and colourful person. Learn to be your own best audience – never feel guilty for needing attention, but appreciate yourself and let yourself blossom under your own applause.

Scorpio Sun / Virgo Moon

In general, you are organised and controlled – at least in the things that matter to you – and you can be intensely private. It is important to you to feel you are in charge of your life, and you are methodical and industrious. Your standards are quite high, and you may never be satisfied with yourself – you may wish to reason away your emotions, or at least assemble them neatly, like socks in a drawer. You are capable of achieving so much, because you go about things in an orderly fashion, and channel your considerable energies in a thoughtful and steady manner. Although you are practical at times, you may seem to live in a world of your own. Why are you always so self-critical? And where did all those 'shoulds' and 'oughts' come from? While you may be excellent at achieving most of your goals, you may still be uneasy about your rawer passions. These are part of your glorious humanity, and they are the powerhouse from which all your beavering gets its energy. Learn to love yourself, warts and all. Sort and label all those passions if you will, but don't reason them away. Use your 'tidying' instincts to throw out all the old rubbish in the shape of value systems that you have taken on board and that make you feel guilty, but have no true meaning for you. That way your life will be organised in a way that works really well for you.

Scorpio Sun / Libra Moon

While you are aware that there is a worm in every apple, you choose not to live with it under your nose – mostly, that is! Of course, there have been times when you may have demolished what was valuable in the name of 'truth' but more usually, understanding people with an uncanny perception, you choose not to upset anyone unnecessarily, and you can achieve harmony and emotional gratification by getting the balance right. Partnerships are important to you, and while you have a keen knowledge of what you need, sometimes you may compromise this in the cause of superficial harmony and peace. Sometimes you try to reason yourself out of uglier emotions, for you are attracted to the beautiful, with a pervading sense of the aesthetic and creative. However, in time you realise that there is no true creativity without access to the deeper wellsprings of humanity, and so you try to be honest with yourself. Always be prepared to brave temporary discord for the sake of authentic relationship, and value your own point of view as well as that of others. It is not enough just to know how you feel – your feelings need a hearing. Make sure you have your own space where you can meditate, reflect, or merely enjoy the things of beauty you cherish.

Appendix 2

ZODIACAL COMPATIBILITY

To assess fully the compatibility of two people the astrologer needs to have the entire chart of each individual, and while Sun-sign factors will be noticeable, there is a legion of other important points to be taken into account. Venus and Mercury are always very close to the Sun, and while these are often in the Sun sign itself, so intensifying its effect, they may also fall in one of the signs lying on either side of your Sun sign. So, as a 'Scorpio' you may have Venus and/or Mercury in Sagittarius or Libra, and this will increase your empathy with these signs. In addition the Moon and all the other planets including the Ascendant and Midheaven need to be taken into account. So if you have always been drawn to Geminis, maybe you have Moon or Ascendant in Gemini.

In order to give a vivid character sketch things have to be stated graphically. You should look for the dynamics at work rather than be too literal about interpretation – for instance, you may find that you are attracted strongly to Aquarians, although you may be aware that you are dissimilar. It is up to the two of you whether a relationship works for it can if you are both committed. Part of that is using the awareness you have to help, not necessarily as a reason for abandoning the relationship. There are always points of compatibility, and we are here to learn from each other.

Appendix 2

On a scale of 1 (worst) to 4 (best), here is a table to assess instantly the superficial compatibility rating between Scorpio and companions:

Scorpio 3	Taurus 3
Sagittarius 2	Gemini 1
Capricorn 3	Cancer 4
Aquarius 2	Leo 1
Pisces 4	Virgo 4
Aries 1	Libra 2

SCORPIO COMPATIBILITIES

Scorpio with Scorpio

You should each know what you are getting, so forewarned is forearmed! The excellent thing about your duo is that you understand the depth and intensity of which the other is capable and which you both require. The danger is that you may become locked in ever more convoluted power struggles. But the making-up is wonderful!

As lovers Sex is profoundly important to you, and while you are both explicitly physical you understand, without necessarily putting this into words, that it is a journey of the soul. While you can match each other for passion, there may be a dimension that is lacking, call it the piquancy of contrast or glimpses of another perspective. If you feel frustrated, the danger is that you will take it out on each other – don't. If you try to transform or control the other or descend into lock-out moods you could be the most gruesome of twosomes. On the other hand, if you protect each other's vulnerability with all the ferocity of which you are capable, if you are loyal, empathic and responsive, together you can make magic. Ms Scorpio realises that this man can at last match her for guts and depth, while Mr Scorpio may develop enough trust to relinquish some control in favour of a passage to transcendence – or you could both be cold as ice. It's up to you – no one knows like two Scorpios how things can be transformed. Make it like you want it.

As friends   Here there is tremendous loyalty and empathy – and you both know the penalty for betrayal! (Only joking – but there is an all-or-nothing quality to Scorpio partnerships of all kinds.) You will support and understand each other until the crack of doom, if you have decided this is your 'best' friend.

As business partners   Both canny, both want control. You could hit the big time or crash and burn. Don't blame each other.

Scorpio with Sagittarius

There is much about the irresponsible Archer that is anathema to Scorpio. However, Scorpio may don armour plating and choose to play Sagittarius's games, if the sex seems good enough. Scorpio will think very carefully before committing emotions to someone so inconsistent, while Sagittarius may become impatient at Scorpionic manipulation. Sagittarius can trundle off once too often, to find something poisonous waiting on his or her return. Sagittarian blissful ignorance of emotional thresholds is no defence!

As lovers   This may be wonderful at the start, for Sagittarius can be ardent and enthusiastic, matching Scorpionic passion. Sagittarius is usually aware of the higher dimensions of sex, and so there may be common ground, although Sagittarius may tend more to philosophy than loss of self in sensual ecstasy. Ms Scorpio finds this man interesting and stimulating, while Mr Scorpio finds Miss Sagittarius charismatic – however, Scorpio will do a lot of checking out before letting the guard down, and Sagittarius may be outraged to discover the diary has been read (there is every chance, thankfully, that

Scorpio will get away with such machinations, for if Sagittarius's diary is found in a different pocket they will merely blame their own scattiness!). This relationship *can* work, if Sagittarius will at least appreciate that he or she has been insensitive and apologise with feeling, and if Scorpio can appreciate the never-failing Sagittarian cheerfulness.

As friends Scorpio appreciates that Sagittarius is great to have around on a wet day, and the side of the Archer that ponders life and its meanings can find common ground with Scorpio's submarine mentality. However, Sagittarius can irritate Scorpio with superficiality, while the Archer can lose patience with it all being so sepulchral.

As business partners Great, if you have your own areas: Sagittarius the salesperson/entrepreneur; Scorpio deals with the money and detection of smelly rats. If forced together too often the differences will tell.

Scorpio with Capricorn

These are one of the leather brogues of zodiac couples – built not for style but to go the distance. Of course, glamour may be a little lacking, but neither of these signs sets much store by the flashy. Capricorn solidity offers much to Scorpionic insecurity, and no one can take jealous assaults with the fortitude of Capricorn. Capricorn, too, is not above getting suspicious, but not to the extent that the partnership can become Macchiavellian. Each can, and does reassure the other.

As lovers This can be very good, for each is very sexually orientated, and the Earthiness of Capricorn can form a sound basis for Scorpionic questing of heights and depths. Ms Scorpio gradually warms to this dependable yet resilient man, while Mr Scorpio appreciates this woman's restrained sensuality. Trouble may set in when Saturnian Capricorn cannot respond to the Scorpion's emotional intensity, which can mean Scorpio feels unloved, while Earthy Capricorn can find the emotional roller-coaster a bit wearing, even for nerves of stone! However, neither of these are quitters and Golden Anniversary time may arrive with you still talking to each other (not *very* chatty, of course, but there is togetherness in monosyllables).

As friends You two can be the best of friends, building your relationship on mutual trust. Capricorn, as the practical half, does keep Scorpio from some of the possible excesses, while Scorpio adds depth to the Goat's appreciation of life.

As business partners Both very shrewd, but perhaps a little over-cautious. A Fire sign on board will add flair.

Scorpio with Aquarius

These two signs really can drive each other mad, but they are so often drawn together that there is no doubt they have much to offer each other. Scorpio may admire Aquarian mental acuity and find all that detachment tantalising. This Water sign just *knows* that no one is *really* that cool and detached, and may spot Aquarian denied emotions while the Air sign, all noble and cerebral, hasn't a clue. Aquarius accuses Scorpio of being irrational and uncivilised – which may have more than a grain of truth. Neither can leave the other be, and a merry time is had by all!

As lovers This may start out very well, for if anyone can stimulate Aquarius to passion it is steamy Scorpio, and sex may be inventive and even volcanic as the two Elements interact. Ms Scorpio finds the coolness and unconventionality of this man irresistible, while Mr Scorpio finds Ms Aquarius tantalising. However, the sheer detachment of Aquarius can be too much, in the long run, for Scorpio, while Aquarius may not be able to handle passion and intimacy, and may long for 'fresh air'. If Scorpio can understand that Aquarius needs to have a concept of the ideas and ideals of the relationship, and that has much to offer in terms of wider perspective, and if Aquarius can appreciate that the heart has its own laws – Scorpio knows about these, and half their own nature is being amputated by disregard of this – this relationship can be truly transforming. It's make or break, and each can grow as a result.

As friends Even without sex there is much that may draw the two of you together, for you each have interests in the fringes of human experience. However, both of you are stubborn, so there may be many arguments.

As business partners Aquarian plans and visions receive their foil in Scorpionic realism and knowledge of human nature. A good combination, but someone else might be needed for the charm and PR.

Scorpio with Pisces

One of the best combinations, Piscean sensitivity can forestall Scorpionic suspicions and emotional pain - no one knows how to keep Scorpio happy better than Pisces, and Scorpionic steadfastness makes Pisces feel secure. Pisces will understand the moods, although it may all become a bit much for them and they may seek some form of escape, which won't help matters! The main drawback to this relationship is that Pisces people are unable, in their heart of hearts, to give themselves totally to anyone or anything, because a part of them belongs to the cosmos. Scorpio knows this, at some level, and may find it hard to cope with.

♏ SCORPIO ♏

As lovers   These two can fall deeply and irretrievably in love, and each is capable of exploring the extremes of physical and emotional ecstasy. Ms Scorpio values the depth and understanding of Mr Pisces, while Mr Scorpio is profoundly attracted to the fathomlessness and femininity of Ms Pisces, which makes him feel he can be understood and loved without having to expose his inner self. Scorpio may feel able to control the relationship, which is true, but only up to a point. When Pisces is finally pushed too far, then he or she can retreat where no one can follow, and become elusive and unreliable, so driving Scorpio to extremes of jealousy. However, this rarely happens, for where Pisces feels cherished and needed and where Pisces understands how the other person is feeling, he or she will put up with almost anything. Scorpio is usually very capable of making Pisces feel secure and wanted.

As friends   Empathy here is usually intense – so much the case that Pisces may be eternally unaware of the Scorpionic sting. There is simply no need for the Scorpion to attack someone who is so genuinely understanding, and Scorpio can be very protective of Pisces. These two may enjoy instinctive rapport and share many interests.

As business partners   This can be very good, for Scorpio has toughness and realism, but is also able to value Pisces' imaginative and intuitive contribution. Scorpio is often better with money.

Scorpio with Aries

Here we have two very passionate people. Scorpio's ruler, before the discovery of Pluto was Mars, shared with Aries, and Scorpio was called the 'night house' of Mars. This gives us a clue as to the contrast between the two signs. While Aries is all up-front assertiveness and enterprise, Scorpio smoulders. Each can wound the other deeply, but while Aries may forget and move on, Scorpio does not. Life can be a running battle or an unforgettable encounter . . . .

As lovers Sex is likely to be red-hot, especially at first. However, Scorpio will find it hard to understand that Aries is really as innocent as he or she seems, and may plot retaliation when Aries is conscious of no crime – despite the fact they have stamped all over every concealed corn Scorpio possesses! Initially, Ms Scorpio warms to the vitality of Mr Aries and Mr Scorpio's conquistadorial tendencies are aroused by Fiery Ms Aries. This relationship does need a lot of work if it isn't to tear everyone to ribbons – and that can include friends and family. Scorpio needs every ounce of understanding to believe that with Aries what you see usually *is* what you get, and Aries must simply learn to count to ten before rushing in causing deep hurt if they do not think. Then it is possible this grande passion could last a lifetime.

As friends Like most relationships between these two signs, we may have one extreme or the other. Either the bond will be intense or you are likely to have little time for each other, rubbing each other up the wrong way all the time. If you do hit it off you will be each other's champion and confidante, so treasure this and never fight dirty.

As business partners Aries may want too much freedom for Scorpio's comfort. Scorpio needs to control everything in the environment that is important to personal security and Arien impulsiveness may be a threat to this. You both have lots of drive – this could work, with mutual respect, and if Aries can bear Scorpio's stranglehold on the purse strings.

Scorpio with Taurus

These two are both extremely sensual. However, with Taurus the drive is primarily towards sensual gratification, and while this may appear to be the case with Scorpio, this Water sign is actually after something much more meaningful. The stubbornness of these two can result in total *impasse*, the annoying thing being that Taurus never even notices Scorpio's manoeuvering, unless it involves denial of sex. Then a rift can develop in the area of main compatibility.

As lovers   If Scorpio is in a mood of sexual experimentation, this can be an unforgettable encounter. A long-term association may result in a stomach-churning, roller-coaster ride that leaves both of these Fixed signs wondering where they have left their insides. Both can be jealous and possessive. Taurus isn't very good at reassuring a probing Scorpio, for the Bull cannot and will not understand what the fuss is about. Of course, it is a different matter when they are left hanging on the line by a vengeful Scorpion. At first Ms Scorpio is drawn to the powerful physical presence of the Taurean male, while Mr Scorpio is fascinated by this lady's sensual ambience. If these two can resolve their differences, there is no sign that can make Scorpio feel safer than Taurus, and Scorpio can, in turn, meet all the Bull's physical needs. Sex is important. Work at the patience and understanding.

As friends   The imperturbable pragmatism of Taurus can be deeply soothing to a tortured Scorpion – or it may seem irrelevantly superficial. If these two do form a bond it may well last a lifetime and long gaps in communication will not sever the ties, for neither sign changes much, except for the times Scorpio undergoes a fundamental transformation. Even then, the solid presence of the Bull can be a reminder that some things can be relied upon in life.

As business partners   Scorpio will value Taurean good sense with money, while Taurus, who may not set much store by intuition, is not above seeing the advantages of Scorpionic penetrative insight when it comes to who to trust in business. As you are both rather slow to warm up, some enterprise may need to be injected from elsewhere.

Scorpio with Gemini

Gemini is, in many ways, the last sign Scorpio would choose, and yet the two are often drawn by the power of their differences. Gemini is light, lively, superficial and cerebral, while Scorpio is dark, given to brooding and emotional depth. Because of this they have much to offer each other, which each may instinctively realise. However, things aren't likely to be comfortable!

As lovers Scorpio may find Gemini very tantalising, and sex is likely to be inventive and varied. Ms Scorpio is mesmerised by the Airy man's gymnastic mind, and may find flirtatious remarks very erotic. Mr Scorpio finds Ms Gemini provocative and witty. Scorpio is sure there are unplumbed depths here (as everywhere), but will be hard put to find them as Gemini flits like a dragonfly over the surface and Scorpio dredges. The best thing these two can do is *talk*. If Scorpionic penetration can find response in Geminian intellectual expertise, the two may come to understand their relationship – Gemini loves to analyse emotions, and Scorpio has plenty of them! One thing is certain – neither of you will ever again find anyone else who is so interesting.

As friends Scorpio is likely to admire Gemini's quick wit, appreciating this can get to the nub of the matter, while Gemini is amazed at Scorpionic tenacity. Surprisingly, there may be shared interests (e.g. psychology) which may cement the friendship. Scorpio must learn not to rely on Gemini being there when needed, and to find emotional support elsewhere, appreciating Gemini for what is on offer.

As business partners This may be excellent, if each can have separate areas. Gemini is a great salesperson, while Scorpio hears the tinkle of skeletons in cupboards.

Scorpio with Cancer

You two will hang in there together like two barnacles, even in an acid bath. Both of you are passionate, committed and private, and both are only too well aware of emotional undercurrents, which means you can hurt each other deeply, give each other the deepest fulfilment and the most cushioning emotional security – which you both so sorely need and are so loathe to admit! This is one of the best zodiacal combinations with much common ground.

As lovers Your sex life can develop into something that is ecstatic and utterly satisfying. Ms Scorpio feels that here is a man who possesses the sensitivity and inherent toughness to match her, while Mr Scorpio warms to the subtle allure and gentle responsiveness of Ms Cancer. You both take a while to warm up, but having gradually learnt to trust you have a relationship that is the depth of a Pacific trench. Of course, we all know that besides the strange and beautiful, much that is terrifying lurks in these depths. You share one trait that could be your downfall – moods. Learn to kiss and make up before the icicles form teeth around the bedroom door.

As friends You will probably understand what the other is feeling before anything has been said, and your friendship could last a lifetime. Sometimes Scorpio can find Cancer a little too timid, but the Scorpion can always understand the reasons for hesitation. Never wound each other – you each know how, but it would be unforgiveable.

As business partners Here the shared caution may be more of a trip wire than a safety net. Enlist a bit of Fire, or that cheque book will turn yellow with age before either of you signs money away!

Appendix 2

Scorpio with Leo

Each of you has the pride of Lucifer, the possessiveness of Othello and the relentlessness of a bulldozer rolling downhill. With all that in common perhaps you ought to get on, and the truth is that you *can*, for you have much to offer each other. However, it is just as likely that you will fight, endlessly.

As lovers   Two intense characters can make for some wonderful sex, for Leo can match Scorpio for passion, on a good day, and Scorpio is so at home with their emotions that this can have a grounding effect on the Lion, who may feel very reassured at being so desired. Ms Scorpio admires the dignity and expressiveness of this larger-than-life man, while Mr Scorpio is drawn to dramatic Ms Leo. This theatrical relationship can be like life on top of the San Andreas fault, as Scorpio hubbles and bubbles and Leo erupts, but feelings run high and are a strong bond. Who wants a boring old life, anyway? Remember what first attracted you – Leo's openness appeals to Scorpio and Scorpionic subtlety appeals to Leo – and keep love alive.

As friends   Leo can ignite Scorpionic faith in life and people – a pale flicker, most of the time – and Scorpio can show Leo hidden depths and nuances. You may be friends for life and mutual champions, in which case Heaven help anyone who criticises either one in the other's hearing – or you could dismiss each other as autocratic and insufferable. You contrast, but you don't have to clash, if you work at appreciation.

As business partners   OK, if you can get through the histrionics. Leo's enthusiasm is a foil for Scorpio's caution. Scorpio must be the moneybags.

♏ SCORPIO ♏

Scorpio with Virgo

Virgo's reputation for prudery is largely unjustified, and in many ways this Earth sign is well suited to intense Scorpio. Both of you present a quiet exterior, but there are often hidden depths to this relationship. Although you go about things in different ways, neither of you accepts face values.

As lovers Sexual passion may run very high, although the two of you are unlikely to paw each other in public. Behind closed doors it is another matter entirely. Ms Scorpio finds the restraint and understated sensuality of Mr Virgo irresistible, while Mr Scorpio is enthralled by the elegant sex appeal of Ms Virgo. The Achilles heel of this relationship can be criticism, for each of you can dish it out but neither can take it. Because you each like to probe every detail, neither may allow the other the privacy so deeply needed. Be tactful and give each other space and autonomy.

As friends You may share conspiratorial tendencies, loving to solve mysteries and make secret plans. Virgo has some sensible comments to offer when Scorpio encounters the periodic emotional morass, while Scorpio can show Virgo that some things defy analysis. Make sure your comments are always positive.

As business partners Quite good, although the secret ambitions of Scorpio may be frustrated by Virgoan insistence on details and systems. PR is best handed over to a Fire or Air sign.

Scorpio with Libra

What could be more different from extreme and vitriolic Scorpio than peaceful, moderate Libra? However, the truth is that there are points of similarity, for each has a passion for justice, although while Libra weighs dispassionately Scorpio is arming for retaliation.

Strangely, this relationship could be one of comrades in arms, where Libra clarifies the issue, Scorpio takes an eye for an eye, and Libra negotiates a truce. If this couple has entertained you handsomely it may be a good idea to include them on your dinner-party list – if you value your social standing!

As lovers While Libra may find Scorpio a little 'heavy', the understanding of Libra often soothes Scorpio, and they make excellent bedmates, where style and refinement meet passion and dimension. This can rise to a wonderful crescendo, if the partners give it time. Libra is great at patiently coaxing the Scorpion to discuss her or his grievances and really listening, but Scorpio may feel that depth is lacking – and let's face it, Libra may become a little nervous around a simmering Scorpio. These two signs have much to offer each other, for Scorpio needs some of that Libran detachment as much as Libra needs the guts and power of Scorpio.

As friends Discussions about human dynamics and ethics may be a common ground, but often Scorpio becomes impatient of Libran lack of commitment and suspects that faultless veneer conceals some spectacular nasties, which is usually untrue, but you try convincing Scorpio! Libra, in turn, finds Scorpio somewhat crude and excessive. Try to give each other a chance.

As business partners Smiling Libra can sell ice-cubes to Eskimos, while Scorpio comes in behind, imposing tough mortgages on the igloos. This combination can be excellent, but needless to say, Scorpio should have the cheque book.

Appendix 3

■ TRADITIONAL ASSOCIATIONS AND TOTEM

Each sign of the zodiac is said to have an affinity with certain colours, plants, stones and other substances. Of course, we cannot be definite about this, for not only do sources vary regarding specific correspondences – we also have the rest of the astrological chart to bear in mind. Some people also believe that the whole concept of such associations is invalid. However, there certainly do seem to be some links between the character of each of the signs and the properties of certain substances. It is up to you to experiment and to see what works for you.

Anything that traditionally links with Scorpio is likely to intensify Scorpionic traits. So if you wish, for some reason, to remain dispassionate and cool, you should steer clear of deep reds, and basil or myrrh essential oils! However, if you want to be your intense, Scorpionic best, it may help to surround yourself with the right stimuli, especially on a down day. Here are some suggestions:

- **Colours** Strong colours, such as wine red, deep green, purple and black. Having said this, it is surprising how many Scorpios prefer to wear neutral colours.
- **Flowers** Gardenia, violet.

- **Metal** Plutonium, iron and steel. Many Scorpios like silver, which has lunar associations.
- **Stones** Kunzite, spinel, ruby, garnet.

Aromatherapy

Aromatherapy uses the healing power of essential oils both to prevent ill health and to maintain good health. Specific oils can sometimes be used to treat specific ailments. Essential oils are concentrated and powerful substances, and should be treated with respect. Buy from a reputable source. *Do not use any oil in pregnancy until you have checked with a reputable source that it is OK (see 'Further Reading'). Do not ingest oils* – they act through the subtle medium of smell, and are absorbed in massage. *Do not place undiluted on the skin.* For massage: Dilute in a carrier oil such as sweet almond or grapeseed, two drops of oil to one teaspoon of carrier. Use in an oil burner, six to ten drops at a time, to fragrance your living area.

Essential oils

- **Basil** A nerve tonic. This will help if you feel tense or anxious. Good also for soothing respiratory infections.
- **Ginger** Warm and spicy, good for relieving aches and pains, colds, 'flu and stomach cramps. Ginger generates a feeling of warmth.
- **Myrrh** This has a musky, secret aroma. It is good for healing many skin conditions, rejuvenating and preserving. It is also anti-inflammatory.
- **Patchouli** Mossy and sensual, patchouli has properties similar to myrrh. A few drops added to shampoo are good for combatting oily hair.

♏ SCORPIO ♏

Naturally you are not restricted to oils ruled by your sign, for in many cases treatment by other oils will be beneficial, and you should consult a reputable source for advice if you have a particular problem. If a problem persists, consult your GP.

Your birth totem

According to the tradition of certain native North American tribes, each of the signs of the zodiac is known by a totem animal. The idea of the totem animal is useful, for animals are powerful, living symbols and they can do much to put us in touch with our potentials. Knowing your totem animal is different from knowing your sign, for your sign is used to define and describe you – as we have been doing in this book – whereas your totem shows you a path of potential learning and growth.

The totem for Scorpio is the Snake, and you also have an affinity with Grizzly Bear and Frog. You were born in the Frost Time. There is a difficulty here, for the North American lore is based on the seasonal cycle. Thus for those of you living in the Southern Hemisphere, it may be worth bearing in mind the totems of your opposite sign, Taurus. These are Beaver, also Eagle and possibly Turtle, although Turtle is for the Earth clan. The Taurean time is called Growing Time.

Snakes represent the cycle of transformation from birth, through sexuality, death and rebirth in the shedding of their skins. The spiralling movement of the snake suggests passage into and out of the manifest world – an ancient and mystical association, from the time of the Stone Age Great Mother. Snake brings wisdom and healing – two snakes are depicted entwining the staff of the cadeuceus, which is the symbol for the healing profession. Snake brings understanding and a sense of timing that comes from a sound identification with the instincts.

Appendix 3

Contacting your totem

You can use visualisation techniques to make contact with the energies of your birth totem. You will need to be very quiet, still and relaxed. Make sure you won't be disturbed. Have a picture of your totem before you, and perhaps burn one of the oils we have mentioned, in an oil burner, to intensify the atmosphere. When you are ready, close your eyes and imagine that you are your totem animal – imagine how it feels, what it smells, sees, hears. What are its feelings, instincts and abilities? Keep this up for as long as you are comfortable, then come back to everyday awareness. Write down your experiences and eat or drink something to ground you. This can be a wonderfully refreshing and mind-clearing exercise, and you may find it inspiring. Naturally, if you feel you have other totem animals – creatures with which you feel an affinity – you are welcome to visualise those. Look out for your totems in the wild – there may be a message for you.

Further reading and resources

Astrology for Lovers, Liz Greene, Unwin, 1986. The title may be misleading, for this is a serious, yet entertaining and wickedly accurate account of the signs. A table is included to help you find your Rising Sign. This book is highly recommended.

Teach Yourself Astrology, Jeff Mayo and Christine Ramsdale, Hodder & Stoughton, 1996. A classic textbook for both beginner and practising astrologer, giving a fresh insight to birth charts through a unique system of personality interpretation.

Love Signs for Beginners, Kristyna Arcarti, Hodder & Stoughton, 1995. A practical introduction to the astrology of romantic relationships, explaining the different roles played by each of the planets and focussing particularly on the position of the Moon at the time of birth.

Star Signs for Beginners, Kristyna Arcarti, Hodder & Stoughton, 1993. An analysis of each of the star signs – a handy, quick reference.

The Moon and You for Beginners, Teresa Moorey, Hodder & Stoughton, 1996. Discover how the phase of the Moon when you were born affects your personality. This book looks at the nine lunar types – how they live, love, work and play, and provides simple tables to enable you to find out your birth phase and which type you are.

The New Compleat Astrologer, Derek and Julia Parker, Mitchell Beazley, 1984. This is a complete introduction to astrology with instructions

Further reading and resources

on chart calculation and planetary tables, as well as clear and interesting descriptions of planets and signs. Including history and reviewing present-day astrology, this is an extensive work, in glossy, hardback form, with colour illustrations.

The Knot of Time: Astrology and the Female Experience, Lindsay River and Sally Gillespie. For personal growth, from a gently feminine perspective, this book has much wisdom.

The Astrology of Self-discovery, Tracy Marks, CRCS Publications, 1985. This book is especially useful for Moon signs.

The Astrologer's Handbook, Francis Sakoian and Louis Acker, Penguin, 1984. This book explains chart calculation and takes the reader through the meanings of signs and planets, with extensive interpretations of planets in signs and houses. In addition, all the major aspects between planets and angles are interpreted individually. A very useful work.

Aromatherapy for Pregnancy and Childbirth, Margaret Fawcett RGN, RM, LLSA, Element, 1993.

The Aromatherapy Handbook, Daniel Ryman, C W Daniel, 1990.

Useful addresses

The Faculty of Astrological Studies

The claim of the Faculty to provide the 'finest and most comprehensive astrological tuition in the world' is well founded. Correspondence courses of a high calibre are offered, leading to the internationally recognised diploma. Evening classes, seminars and summer schools are taught, catering for the complete beginner to the most experienced astrologer. A list of trained consultants can be supplied on request, if you wish for a chart interpretation. For further details telephone (UK code) 0171 700 3556 (24-hour answering service); or fax 0171 700 6479. Alternatively, you can write, with SAE, to: Ref. T. Moorey, FAS., BM7470, London WC1N 3XX, UK.

Educational

California Institute of Integral Studies, 765 Ashbury St, San Francisco, CA 94117. Tel: (415) 753-6100

Kepler College of Astrological Arts and Sciences, 4518 University Way, NE, Suite 213, Seattle, WA 98105. Tel: (206) 633-4907

Robin Armstrong School of Astrology, Box 5265, Station 'A', Toronto, Ontario, M5W 1N5, Canada. Tel: (416) 923-7827

Vancouver Astrology School, Astraea Astrology, Suite 412, 2150 W Broadway, Vancouver, V6K 4L9, Canada. Tel: (604) 536-3880

The Southern Cross Academy of Astrology, PO Box 781147, Sandton, SA 2146 (South Africa) Tel: 11-468-1157; Fax: 11-468-1522

Periodicals

American Astrology Magazine, PO Box 140713, Staten Island, NY 10314-0713. e-mail: am.astrology@genie.gies,com

The Journal of the Seasons, PO Box 5266, Wellesley St, Auckland 1, New Zealand. Tel/fax: (0)9-410-8416

The Federation of Australian Astrologers Bulletin, PO Box 159, Stepney, SA 5069. Tel/fax: 8-331-3057

Aspects, PO Box 2968, Rivonia, SA 2128, (South Africa) Tel: 11-864-1436

Realta, The Journal of the Irish Astrological Association, 4 Quay Street, Galway, Ireland. Available from IAA, 193, Lwr Rathmines Rd, Dublin 6, Ireland.

Astrological Association, 396 Caledonian Road, London, N1 1DN. Tel: (UK code) 0171 700 3746; Fax: 0171 700 6479. Bi-monthly journal issued.